Confronting Policy Challenges of the Great Recession

Confronting Policy Challenges of the Great Recession

Lessons for Macroeconomic Policy

Eskander Alvi
Editor

2017

W.E. Upjohn Institute for Employment Research
Kalamazoo, Michigan

Library of Congress Cataloging-in-Publication Data

Names: Alvi, Eskander, 1956- editor.
Title: Confronting policy challenges of the Great Recession : lessons for
  macroeconomic policy / Eskander Alvi, editor.
Description: Kalamazoo, Michigan : W.E. Upjohn Institute for Employment Research,
  2017. | Includes index.
Identifiers: LCCN 2017044709 | ISBN 9780880996365 (pbk. : alk. paper) | ISBN
  0880996366 (pbk. : alk. paper) | ISBN 9780880996372 (hardcover : alk. paper) |
  ISBN 0880996374 (hardcover : alk. paper)
Subjects: LCSH: Recessions. | Monetary policy. | Economic policy.
Classification: LCC HB3716.C66 2017 | DDC 339.5—dc23 LC record available at
  https://lccn.loc.gov/2017044709

The facts presented in this study and the observations and viewpoints expressed are
the sole responsibility of the authors. They do not necessarily represent positions of
the W.E. Upjohn Institute for Employment Research.

Cover design by Carol A.S. Derks.
Index prepared by Diane Worden.
Printed in the United States of America.
Printed on recycled paper.

Contents

Acknowledgments

The chapters in this book are based on presentations made at the annual Werner Sichel Economics Lecture Series, hosted by the Western Michigan University (WMU) Department of Economics during the 2014–2015 academic year. The series is made possible through financial support from the W.E. Upjohn Institute for Employment Research and WMU. It is named for Dr. Werner Sichel, who retired in 2005 after 45 years of teaching at WMU.

1
The Great Recession, Fallout, and What We Learned

Eskander Alvi
Western Michigan University

The Great Recession (December 2007–June 2009) roiled financial markets around the world and caused significant damage to the global economy on a scale that is comparable only to the Great Depression. Starting in the United States with the collapse of housing prices, its reach expanded quickly to financial markets inside and outside the country and soon swamped the international economy. The outsized losses in the broader financial sector and the rapid deterioration of the pace of aggregate economic activity posed extraordinary challenges on many fronts. Not since the 1930s have policymakers been confronted with such near-catastrophic events.

This volume presents five chapters on macro policy challenges in the Great Recession from some of the country's most distinguished economists who came to Kalamazoo, Michigan, as part of the fifty-first Werner Sichel Lecture Series (2014–2015), which was sponsored jointly by the Department of Economics at Western Michigan University and the W.E. Upjohn Institute for Employment Research. The chapters included here follow from their presentations. The idea is that confronting the policy challenges will encourage more discussion and research to better instruct future policy in dealing with comparable adversities.

It is now well understood that the Great Recession was caused by a housing bubble that was enabled by easy access to credit and a belief that housing prices would not fall. On the supply side, lenders secured additional funds by selling their mortgages, which fed into strong incentives to lend. Securitization of mortgages became common and created an aggressive lending cycle that started with lending to home buyers, followed by selling the mortgages, which were then securitized and sold to investors, leaving lenders with more funds to

1

advance to other home buyers. Since the loan originators would pass on the mortgages, they had little interest in making sure that the borrowers were financially sound. Subprime mortgages that resulted were often bundled with prime ones in complex ways, which made the risks less transparent. Furthermore, the credit rating agencies deemed the securities worthy, giving them a seal of approval as a safe investment product. The near-collapse of the financial system wreaked havoc on itself and the larger global economy. As Reinhart and Rogoff (2009) note in their well-known research, output losses associated with financial crises can be dreadful and persistent. The 2008 recession lived up to that description.

The authors in this book describe the unprecedented events and the often-extraordinary policies put in place to limit the damage and turn the economy around. Not surprisingly, some policies worked well while others barely made a dent. An analysis of the many lessons and encounters, successes and failures, will surely offer fresh perspectives on how to manage the economy in a future crisis of comparable proportion. While some research has been conducted on the lessons of the Great Recession, an appreciation of the accompanying challenges adds value and enriches policy content. The hindsight afforded by the Great Recession is invaluable, and in the following five chapters we hope to underscore the main issues policymakers faced.

When beset by a crisis, we are prone to look for precedents in judging what kinds of policies are likely to be effective. Barry Eichengreen offers that viewpoint by drawing analogies between the Great Depression and the Great Recession and the lessons learned. He also makes a connection between politics and fiscal policies, drawing on historical precedence. Even in the case of monetary policy, though the central bank has much autonomy, the Federal Reserve worries about any potential compromise of independence if it is at odds with Congress or the prevailing political sentiment. The challenges arising from the political direction is a common theme in the book, a view that is well positioned by Gary Burtless. No discussion of the Great Recession is complete without the extraordinary policies taken by the Federal Reserve. Donald Kohn, who was the vice chair at the central bank from 2006 to 2010, provides an explicit description of how the Federal Reserve dealt with the crisis. Another common theme is the sluggish recovery. Laurence Ball and his coauthors take on the lower trend path of potential GDP following the 2008 recession and suggests fiscal stimulus to close that gap, arguing that this could be achieved without increasing the public debt. The effects of the Great Recession quickly went international, with financial crises outside the country often appearing to be worse than in the United States. Kathryn Dominguez looks at the financial and trade connections to ask if the foreign shocks were responsible for the slow recovery in the United States.

In Chapter 2, Eichengreen presents a historical perspective on lessons learned from past crises and how they are applied—and often misapplied—in subsequent periods of turmoil. The major precedent—the Great Depression of the 1930s—offered a variety of guidelines for policymakers, from preventing bank runs to providing emergency lending and allowing stimulus on the fiscal side.

Policy did succeed in applying some lessons learned on many fronts—on the financial side, it prevented a large-scale bank run, aggressively lowering the federal funds rate and provisioning plenty of liquidity through both quantitative easing when rates could not go any lower and two fiscal stimulus packages to prop up spending. But there was also failure in a few critical areas, the most notable being the failure of Lehman Brothers. This seriously compromised the lender of last resort obligation that the Fed normally maintains and in turn created an extraordinary degree of uncertainty regarding which financial institution might fail next. Both Eichengreen and Burtless point to the political climate of blame that may have been partly responsible—the public perceived that the Federal Reserve was bailing out large banks responsible for bringing about financial chaos, while homeowners with bad mortgages and folks on Main Street were left in the lurch.

The central bank's large-scale purchase of mortgage-backed securities was also viewed with apprehension in some quarters. There was concern that it looked much like the elements leading up to the housing bubble. To be sure, the housing market after the collapse did benefit from the injection of direct liquidity, money that would normally not flow in that direction because of extraordinary risks. Restoring supply offered a much-needed lifeline to the mortgage and refinance market. Political disenfranchisement aside, it is also hard to deny that a recognition of moral hazard was at play, that the Federal Reserve would not try enough to corral a potential buyer for Lehman Brothers. Following the purchase of Bear Stearns by JP Morgan Chase with a $30 billion loan from the Federal Reserve, one wonders how much more a prospective buyer would require and whether that amount would be forthcoming.

The second shortcoming both Eichengreen and Burtless refer to is that policymakers did not gauge the magnitude of the missteps. Once Lehman Brothers failed, the financial sector entered a renewed vicious phase of panic and uncertainty, the extent of which policy formulators had not anticipated. After the fact, though, central banks in the United States and Europe worked hard to restore confidence, sparing no resource to shore up the ailing institutions, which suggests they may have miscalculated the fallout from Lehman's demise. Perhaps because Lehman was not a depository bank, the lessons from the Great Depression did not quite instruct policy in the Great Recession. A related deficiency, though on a different scale, was that while a housing bubble was recognized early on, the scope and magnitude of the damage it would bring to the real economy was not. The common policy view was that any macro damage from the housing debacle would be limited. It was not fully appreciated that extensive securitization of mortgages had spread the risks well beyond the housing market. Because of the ease of securitizing, lenders had an incentive to lend aggressively and pass on the risks to buyers and holders of mortgage-backed securities. Such risks were not properly priced, which became apparent only after the collapse of house prices. In sum, policymakers had underestimated the risks of their own missteps, as with the failure of Lehman, and did not properly identify the broadening macro risks arising from the housing market.

The third shortcoming was that although averting a disaster on the scale and enormity of the Great Depression was reason for gratification, that success planted the seeds for policy reversion. Once the economy had stabilized with 10 percent unemployment and growth resumed, although tepid, policymakers breathed a sigh of relief and eased their policy efforts too soon. Eichengreen and Burtless argue that at this juncture the urgency for a continuation of policy receded and deficit and debt worries surfaced. In the United States, a $1.2 trillion spending cut over 10 years was approved in 2011, the Bush tax cuts elapsed, and the sequester—8.5 percent cut in federal spending across the board— was put in place in 2013. Eichengreen argues that the turn to austerity was even more pronounced in Europe, with euro area deficits falling sharply in 2012, despite the return to a recession, while in the U.K. its government turned to fiscal consolidation. Central banks also became reticent after the first stint of victory. The Federal Reserve was cautious in expanding its unconventional measures, waiting until its third round of quantitative easing to make open-ended asset purchases. In 2010 the European Central Bank began to phase out unconventional measures, followed by two premature interest rate increases in 2011.

In Chapter 3, Burtless considers the political fallout from the recession and the subsequent challenges for policy in generating an appropriate pace of recovery. He argues that while monetary policy was active, the fiscal side was rather restrained. Following two fiscal stimulus packages, one in late 2008 and the other in early 2009, there were heightened concerns of unsustainable government debt and a severe public backlash. The perception was that the dollars were being misused to bail out large banks and that the large deficits would be ruinous to the economy. To be sure, the Troubled Asset Relief Program did involve the Treasury buying stocks of distressed financial corporations, but the amount was a fairly small percentage of the overall fiscal stimulus, and in fact, the Treasury did not lose money on this particular undertaking. Nonetheless, political sentiment did not support any additional stimulus even though it gradually became clear that the recession was more severe than originally thought. Burtless also observes that once the financial sector stabilized, with the panic there retreating, the willingness to pass any additional stimulus to reduce unemployment simply dissipated. This reaction is not unusual, Burtless notes in comparing with events in some Western European countries that had high but stable unemployment rates in the 1980s. Once the threat of layoffs ebbs, the motivation to pass new measures to prop up employment also withers.

The institutional setup of fiscal and monetary policies is different. With monetary decision-making delegated to mostly seven voting members of the Federal Reserve Board, policy actions are usually swift. Fiscal policy, in contrast, is determined in the political arena with wider debate and requires approval of both houses of Congress. This often leads to delays and lags. The mix of fast-acting monetary policy with unhurried fiscal policy is generally a good balance. When a major shock like the Great Depression or the Great Recession strikes, however, monetary policy alone may not suffice, and promptness on the fiscal side may be warranted. With interest rates at zero, this was clearly such a scenario. Burtless argues that, with fiscal policy passage subject to political jostling, even in times of great need, as in the Great Recession, the prospect of stimulus can be tardy and unreliable. Additionally, the window of action is often short and closes once the peril of rising layoffs has passed, even though the unemployment rate can remain high. This challenge that Burtless identifies clearly bears recognizing as a constraint on policy timing and possible options for fiscal action.

Monetary policy played a key role in stabilizing the economy. In Chapter 4, Donald Kohn describes the new and not-so-new policies that were put in place. One of the challenges he describes was that institutions in the financial maelstrom were not banks. Securitization, often involving subprime mortgages, had drawn in a variety of financial institutions that did not take deposits and therefore were not subject to close supervision. With subprime mortgages packaged in obscure ways, it was difficult to know where the losses would ultimately accrue following the collapse of the housing market. The feedback between the financial and the real sectors meant financial institutions under stress needed to sell assets, often at fire-sale prices, which would drive down asset prices, including house prices, and increase foreclosures, which would further adversely impact the financial sector. Kohn notes that the central bank was not particularly equipped to deal with such a crisis. Under the Federal Reserve Act of 1913, the Fed is not able to directly lend to households and businesses, but it could act in the financial market to reduce the stress and end the fire sale of assets, which would be a relief to both Wall Street and Main Street. To stop the financial implosion, in 2008 the Fed started to lend to nonbank institutions, something it had not done since the 1930s. This broad provisioning included broker-dealers, money market funds, issuers of commercial paper, and buyers of securitized debt.

Securitization also spread the risks to foreign banks through their purchase of securitized debts that were funded by short-term deposits and borrowings in foreign currencies that were later converted to dollars in swap markets. With the crisis deepening, access to swaps became difficult so they had to bid directly for dollars, which put upward pressure on interest rates. To ease the situation the Fed created central bank foreign currency liquidity swaps—it directly lent dollars to foreign central banks so that they could lend where appropriate to their banks. The extension of risks to nonbanks and foreign financial institutions posed particularly acute challenges for policymakers.

A well-known special challenge facing the central bank was posed by having reached the zero lower bound—the federal funds rate could not be lowered. This was possibly the biggest hurdle for monetary policy. In late 2008 and early 2009, the Fed purchased long-term assets composed of government bonds and mortgage-backed securities. This came to be known as quantitative easing. The Fed first bought mortgage securities in 1971, following legislation that amended section 14(b) of the Federal Reserve Act, which allowed the central bank to buy and sell in the open market mortgage securities that were fully guaranteed by an agency of the U.S. government. When Congress passed that legislation, essentially to ease funding in the housing market, the central bank was uncomfortable in that role, and in 1981 made the last purchase of agency debt before the Great Recession (Haltom and Sharp 2014). The size of asset purchases in the Great Recession, including that of mortgage securities, is unprecedented. However, as Kohn points out, this was an example of a policy that was in the books but long remained dormant, and was put to vigorous use in this recession. It could be argued, by comparison with the 1970s, that the central bank was easing from a situation of exigency rather than normalcy and was evidently less reluctant in exercising that option.

The Federal Reserve also introduced forward guidance—promising to keep the Fed funds rate near the floor for prolonged periods, or until certain inflation and unemployment targets were met. This effectively tethered the future Fed funds rate and removed any perceived upward bias from the central bank's actions going forward. The combination of asset purchase and forward guidance kept longer-term interest rates low and favorably impacted asset prices, including house prices, and encouraged consumer and business spending. Some of the monetary policy measures discussed here started under Fed Chair Ben Benanke and continued under the stewardship of Chair Janet Yellen.

It is useful to note that in the variety of efforts to stabilize the economy, the Fed did not deviate from its usual inflation and unemployment targets—2 percent and full-employment, though it has been argued by some economists that a higher inflation target would provide a stronger boost to aggregate demand. Perhaps the Fed was not comfortable altering the key anchor of monetary policy, an action that would signal a different policy regime and risk confusion about its commitment to low inflation. On the unemployment side, with the natural rate being strictly unknown, the Fed showed a willingness to continue with low interest rates until inflation reached its threshold, rather than raise rates once the unemployment rate reached a predetermined level. This approach let the actual unemployment rate reach 4.3 percent in May 2017.

Kohn argues that communicating the purpose and scope of the policies turned out to be a serious challenge—it was difficult to explain that the Federal Reserve was not bailing out failing institutions but rather providing liquidity to keep the banking and the larger financial system functional. Confusion among the public and in Congress created suspicion and made it difficult to execute policy as needed. It would have been helpful to have had a process to explain the scope of the problem and what has to be done and why, possibly along the lines of the Fed chair directly communicating to the public via the media, something Bernanke had done on a couple of occasions.

In the aftermath of the Great Recession, GDP growth remained sluggish. The disappointing recovery is central to Chapter 5, by Laurence Ball, J. Bradford DeLong, and Lawrence H. Summers. The authors focus on potential GDP and note that its revision was noticeably below the counterpart based on pre-2008 trends, about 7 percent lower, and that estimates by Reifschneider, Wascher, and Wilcox (2013) and the Congressional Budget Office (2014) suggest that about two-thirds of the loss was permanent in nature. In the face of high unemployment and the economy's infrastructure in need of upgrade and repair, the authors propose closing this potential GDP gap by use of fiscal measures. Their choice of fiscal makes good sense given that monetary policy had reached the zero lower bound. In that liquidity trap scenario, an argument is made that a properly designed stimulus would likely reduce rather than increase the debt burden, the logic being that a stimulus would directly raise revenue and in turn lower the debt/GDP ratio, create positive supply effects of public investment, and possibly lead to reductions in real interest costs arising from an increase in expected inflation. Additionally, the debt problem that is normally associated with tax cuts would be mitigated by the hysteresis effects of rising output and employment. Thus, Ball and his coauthors make the forceful argument that with interest rates so low, crowding out would not dilute the expansionary effort and a tax cut would pay for itself.

Referring to some simple calculations by DeLong and Summers (2012), Ball et al. reason that a hysteresis parameter of 0.05 (a $1.00

increase in current output having a positive effect of $0.05 on potential output) via investment, employment, and other favorable effects would suffice in leaving the national debt unchanged in the face of a tax break. The policy challenge here is that with interest rates at their historic lows, this would be a great opportunity for the government to cut taxes and borrow to fund infrastructure. But the political process that is essential to the tax and spend changes may not cooperate, leaving the central bank to continue to assume almost singlehandedly the task of lifting the economy.

The Great Recession started in the United States but spread to other countries through financial and trade linkages. A high degree of financial integration between developed countries meant a synchronous effect of the U.S. financial fallout on other countries. Trade was a second channel that transmitted the adverse consequence across nations. In Chapter 6, Kathryn M.E. Dominguez also notes that the recession was especially severe because of its financial origins, pointing to research by Reinhart and Rogoff (2010), who document the vicious effects on the economy compared to other kinds of recessions. In an integrated system, this can be disastrous both in the size of the downturn and its duration, as exemplified by the Great Depression. Fortunately, in the Great Recession both fiscal and monetary policy were aggressive, which limited the downside. However, on the issue of recovery, she notes, the Great Recession seriously lagged compared to its predecessors (recoveries across the past 11 recessions).

Dominguez maintains that one reason for the weak revival was unfavorable transnational effects. Whereas the United States was weak, the rest of the world was weaker. What appeared to be the beginning of a healthy rebound near the end of 2009 proved to be too optimistic. Europe's financial and fiscal difficulties were becoming full blown, and by 2011 the tsunami and earthquake in Japan and the fiscal impasse in the United States led to considerable revisions of growth forecasts. Japan's return to recession in 2013 and again in 2014, combined with the Russian ruble crisis, created enough downside momentum to limit growth in the United States. To examine the reasons for the slow recovery, Dominguez and Shapiro (2013) use forecast revisions and narrative information from contemporaneous news reports. They find that shocks originating from Europe were the cause between 2010 and 2012. Updating the narrative evidence through 2014 and including a broader group of countries, Dominguez finds that the focus shifts from the United States in 2008–2009 to the Eurozone in 2010, Asia in 2011, and Russia in 2014.

Transmission of shocks across borders creates a special kind of vulnerability and poses a challenge for policy. During the recession, there was some cooperation between the Federal Reserve and major central banks. An example, as mentioned earlier, was the establishment of swap lines, which several foreign banks used. But more general coordination is tricky, since shocks have diverse origins and require different policy responses that are not easy to complement. The tsunami in Japan in 2011 required a very geographically targeted fiscal response by the Japanese government, while bank bailouts in Southern Europe involved the European Union, the European Central Bank, and the International Monetary Fund. The low interest rate policy in the United States clearly helped, but it would be difficult to argue that Federal Reserve should lower rates because of the negative external events, though perhaps the timing of any change in interest policy can be amenable.

The chapters presented here offer an account of the lessons and concurrent challenges faced by policymakers in the 2008 recession. While the lessons discussed are mostly economic, they are almost always seen by both policymakers and the public through the lens of history, politics, and institutions. This often made navigating the course difficult in the recession and presented additional hurdles. One of the contributions of this book is not only a better understanding of the lessons but also of their nuances, limitations, and boundaries. This balance, it is hoped, will better guide future policy in situations of similar distress.

References

Congressional Budget Office. 2014. "Revisions to CBO's Projection of Potential Output Since 2007." Washington, DC: CBO. http://www.cbo.gov/sites/default/files/cbofiles/attachments/45150-PotentialOutput.pdf (accessed April 4, 2017).

DeLong, J. Bradford, and Lawrence H. Summers. 2012. "Fiscal Policy in a Depressed Economy." In *Brookings Papers on Economic Activity*, 2, David H. Romer and Justin Wolfers, eds. Washington, DC: Brookings Institution, pp. 233–274.

Dominguez, Kathryn M.E., and Matthew Shapiro. 2013. "Forecasting the Recovery from the Great Recession: Is This Time Different?" *American Economic Review: Papers and Proceedings* 103(3): 147–152.

Haltom, Renee, and Robert Sharp. 2014. "The First Time the Fed Bought GSE Debt." Economic Brief No. EB14-04. Richmond, VA: Federal Reserve Bank of Richmond.

Reifschneider, Dave, William Wascher, and David Wilcox. 2013. "Aggregate Supply in the United States: Recent Developments and Implications for the Conduct of Monetary Policy." FEDS Working Paper 2013-77. Washington, DC: Federal Reserve Board.

Reinhart, Carmen M., and Kenneth S. Rogoff. 2009. "The Aftermath of Financial Crises." *American Economic Review* 99(2): 466–472.

2

The Great Depression
and the Great Recession
in a Historical Mirror

Barry Eichengreen
University of California, Berkeley

History is a lens through which we—the public and elected and appointed officials—view current problems. The logic of historical analogy is never more compelling than during crises, as there is no time for careful analytical reasoning and no time for building formal models or testing them for fitness to data. In such circumstances, the influence of reasoning by analogy, particularly historical analogy, is considerable. For example, foreign policy specialists point to the powerful influence of the Munich analogy in President Truman's decision to intervene in Korea.[1] Or, think of the power of the analogy between 9/11 and Pearl Harbor, for which a Google search produces nearly 100,000 hits.

So it was with the Great Recession of 2008–2009 and the Great Depression of 1929–1933, the two great macroeconomic crises of the past century. There is no doubt that conventional wisdom about the earlier episode, which is referred to colloquially as "the lessons of the Great Depression," powerfully shaped and informed the response to the crisis of 2008–2009.[2]

The decisions of policymakers were powerfully shaped and informed by received wisdom about the mistakes of their predecessors. In the 1930s when the crisis hit, those predecessors had succumbed to the protectionist temptation. They had cut public spending at the worst possible time and failed to stabilize the money supply. Neglecting their responsibility for financial stability, they had failed to provide emergency liquidity to the banking system. The result was collapsing banks, collapsing prices, collapsing trade, and collapsing activity—in a phrase, the great macroeconomic catastrophe of modern times.

That this economic crisis reflected disastrous but avoidable policy failures became conventional wisdom, courtesy of influential analyses from economists such as Milton Friedman and Anna Schwartz, whose book *Monetary History of the United States* devoted a 110-page chapter to the episode they dubbed "The Great Contraction" (Friedman and Schwartz 1963). In 2008, heeding the lessons of this earlier episode, policymakers vowed to do better. If their predecessors' failure to provide emergency liquidity had produced a cataclysmic banking and financial crisis, then this time they would flood the markets with liquidity and otherwise provide emergency assistance to the banks. If the failure of those predecessors to stabilize the money supply had resulted in a destructive deflation, then this time they would cut interest rates and expand central bank balance sheets. If efforts to balance budgets had worsened the earlier slump, then this time they would apply fiscal stimulus instead.

As a result of this very different response, unemployment in the United States peaked in 2010 at just 10 percent. This was still painfully high, to be sure, but it was far below the catastrophic 24 percent scaled in the Great Depression. This time failed banks numbered in the hundreds, not thousands. While dislocations were widespread, the utter collapse of financial markets, as in the 1930s, was successfully averted.

And what was true of the United States was true also of other countries. Every unhappy country is unhappy in its own way, and there were varying degrees of economic unhappiness starting in 2008. But, a few ill-starred European countries notwithstanding, that unhappiness did not rise to 1930s levels. Because policy was better, the decline in output and employment was less steep, the social dislocations were fewer, and the pain and suffering were less.

Unfortunately, this happy narrative of sage policy informed by "the lessons of history" is a bit too positive. For one thing, it is hard to square with the failure to anticipate the risks. As Queen Elizabeth II famously asked on a visit to the London School of Economics in 2008: "Why did no one see it coming?" (Pierce 2008). Some economists later claimed that they had seen "it" coming (*Telegraph* 2009), but they actually warned of crises that did not occur, like a collapse of the dollar, or issued only vague warnings and without pointing to specific risks.

That even specialists on financial crises did not sound louder warnings—there's my mea culpa—suggests adopting a somewhat less critical posture toward officials in the 1920s for failing to anticipate and head off the risks that resulted in their crisis. Our failure reflects what psychologists refer to as "continuity bias," the subconscious tendency to believe that the future will resemble the relatively recent past (Omer and Alon 1994).[3] It reflects peer pressure to conform and the costs of being ostracized if, for example, you criticized Alan Greenspan's financial stewardship at Jackson Hole in 2005, as one academic was reckless enough to do (Rajan 2005). It reflects the power of a dominant ideology, in this case the ideology of market efficiency and financial liberalization (Patomaki 2009; Suarez and Kolodny 2011). And it reflects the influence of money politics—the influence of big financial institutions, through their political contributions and the revolving door between Wall Street and Washington—in shaping the policy debate (Igan and Mishra 2011; Igan, Mishra, and Tressel 2011; Mian, Sufi, and Trebbi 2010).

Ultimately, however, I would argue that the roots of this failure to see the recent crisis coming lay in the same progressive narrative of the Great Depression. Entirely correctible flaws of collective decision making, that narrative explained, had been responsible for the inability of contemporaries to appreciate the risks to stability in the 1920s and then for their failure to deal effectively with the consequences in the 1930s. Modern-day policymakers had learned from the mistakes of their predecessors. Scientific central banking informed by a rigorous framework of inflation targeting now reduced economic and financial volatility and prevented serious imbalances. Advances in supervision and regulation limited financial excesses. Deposit insurance, put in place in response to the experience of the 1930s, had eliminated the danger of bank runs and financial panics. Conventional wisdom about the Great Depression, that it was caused by avoidable policy failures, was itself conducive to the belief that those failures could be and, indeed, had been corrected. It followed that no comparable crisis was possible now. All of which we now know was dreadfully wrong.

Part of the problem is that we—in this case I mean we economic historians—had always done a better job of explaining the course of the Great Depression than we had in explaining its onset.[4] We had failed to highlight how rapid financial innovation had combined with inadequate regulation and lax monetary policy to create dangerous financial fragilities.[5] We had failed to explain how capital flows to one half of Europe from the other half of Europe and the rest of the world had set up that continent for a fall.[6] We had failed to explain how the naïve belief that advances in scientific central banking had rendered crises a thing of the past, which led contemporaries to discount the risks to financial stability (however, see Barber [1985]). We had failed to explain how a long period of stability—in the 1920s they called it "the New Era" rather than, as recently, the Great Moderation, although the underlying phenomenon was fundamentally the same—encouraged excessive risk taking and empowered those who argued against stricter regulation.[7] Recent experience suggests the need to write this history more carefully. Had we done so earlier, we might have seen more clearly how the same factors were at work in the early twenty-first century.

The fateful decision to let Lehman Brothers fail—the single event that most threatened the stability of global financial markets—also suggests looking at the 1920s differently. Lehman failed because it was insolvent—because its managers had made bad bets. It failed because there were doubts about whether the Fed and Treasury had the legal authority to rescue it.[8] But it also failed because policymakers wanted to make a statement. Having bailed out Bear Stearns six months earlier, they were eager to signal that not everyone would be rescued. And they wanted to shield themselves from criticism from politicians that they were too quick to bail out troubled banks.[9]

Because they lived through this experience, future historians are likely to write the history of the Great Depression differently. They will be reminded that the banking crises of the 1930s reflected not only the fact that central banks and governments failed to appreciate the need to act as lenders of last resort, but, as with Lehman Brothers, their concern with moral hazard and wish to push back against political criticism. The great banking crisis of early 1933 resulted from the failure of the Reconstruction Finance Corporation to rescue Henry Ford's Guardian Group of banks, unleashing a panic that engulfed first the state of Michigan and then the rest of the country.[10] In fact, that decision reflected the criticism to which U.S. politicians, from President Herbert Hoover on down, had been subjected for rescuing Central Republic Trust, the bank of former Vice President (and former Reconstruction Finance Corporation head) Charles Dawes, six months earlier (Vickers 2011). We are reminded that this instinctual desire to "teach them a lesson," to play financial hardball, especially when doing so is a way for officials to rescue their reputations, is deeply ingrained.

There was also the failure to anticipate how disruptive the failure of Lehman Brothers would be. Here too I would blame the "lessons of the Great Depression." The conventional narrative about the Depression focused on the disruptive impact of bank failures and runs by retail depositors.[11] Lehman was not a deposit-taking bank; it did not have retail depositors.[12] Therefore, the conclusion followed, its failure couldn't pose such serious problems.

This view, informed by the lessons of the Great Depression, was why the Basel Accord setting capital standards for internationally active financial institutions focused on commercial banks. Deposit insurance, which was supposed to prevent bank runs, focused on commercial banks. Regulation generally focused on commercial banks. This focus neglected the shadow banking system of investment banks, hedge funds, money market funds, commercial paper issuers, and securitizers. It ignored Lehman's derivatives positions. It ignored the fact that wholesale creditors could effectively run on the bank. The result was the decision to allow the uncontrolled failure of Lehman Brothers, which in my view was the single most serious mistake of the financial crisis.

At this point policymakers realized that they had a situation on their hands—that the U.S. and world economies were on the verge of another Great Depression. The leaders of the advanced industrial countries quickly issued a joint statement that no systematically significant financial institution would be allowed to fail. American International Group (AIG) was bailed out, albeit not on terms that satisfied everyone concerned.[13] A reluctant U.S. Congress passed the Troubled Asset Relief Program on the second try, to aid the banking and financial system. Gordon Brown assembled the Group of Twenty countries in London in February 2009 to produce their so-called "Trillion Dollar Package" of coordinated fiscal-stimulus measures.[14] One after another, governments took steps to provide capital and liquidity to distressed financial institutions. Central banks flooded financial markets with liquidity. Policymakers congratulated themselves that they had avoided another Great Depression.[15]

Yet the results of these policy initiatives were decidedly less than triumphal. Postcrisis recovery in the United States was lethargic. It proceeded at less than half the pace of a normal recovery, a couple of quarters of exceptionally rapid growth in the middle of 2014 notwithstanding to the contrary. Europe did even worse, experiencing a double-dip recession and renewed crisis starting in 2010.

This was not the successful stabilization and vigorous recovery promised by those who had learned the lessons of history.[16] The reasons why are no mystery. Starting in 2010 the United States and Europe took a hard right turn toward austerity. Spending under the American Recovery and Investment Act, President Obama's stimulus program, peaked in fiscal year 2010 and then headed steadily downward. In the summer of 2011, the Obama Administration and the Congress then agreed to $1.2 trillion of spending cuts to be implemented over 10 years. In 2013 came expiry of the Bush tax cuts; the end of the temporary reduction in employee contributions to the Social Security Trust Fund; and the sequester (the across-the-board 8.5 percent cut in federal government spending). All this took a big bite out of spending, aggregate demand, and economic growth.[17]

In Europe the turn was even more dramatic. In Greece, where spending was out of control, a dose of austerity was clearly required. But the adjustment program on which the country embarked starting in 2010 under the watchful eyes of the European Commission, the European Central Bank (ECB), and the International Monetary Fund was unprecedented. It required the Greek government to reduce spending and raise taxes by an extraordinary 16 percent of GDP over four years—in effect, to eliminate more than one-seventh of all spending in the Greek economy. The governments of the euro area as a whole cut budget deficits modestly in 2011 and then sharply in 2012, despite the fact that the currency area was back in recession and other forms of spending were stagnant. Even the United Kingdom, which had the flexibility afforded by a national currency and a national central bank, embarked on an ambitious program of fiscal consolidation, cutting government spending and raising taxes by a cumulative 5 percent of GDP.[18]

Central banks, having taken a variety of exceptional steps in the crisis, were similarly anxious to return to business as usual. The Fed undertook three rounds of quantitative easing (QE)—multimonth purchases of Treasury bonds and mortgage-backed securities—but hesitated to ramp up those purchases even further despite an inflation rate that undershot its 2 percent target and growth that continued to disappoint for three additional years. Not until QE3 did it finally make the kind of open-ended commitment sufficient to vanquish the threat of deflation once and for all.[19]

And if the Fed was reluctant to do more, the ECB was eager to do less. In 2010 it prematurely concluded that recovery was at hand and started phasing out its nonstandard measures. In 2011 it raised interest rates twice. Anyone seeking to understand why the European economy failed to recover and instead dipped a second time need look no further.

What lessons, historical or otherwise, informed this extraordinary turn of events? For central banks there was, as always, deeply ingrained fear of inflation. That fear was nowhere deeper than in Germany, given memories of hyperinflation in 1923. German fear now translated into European policy, given the Bundesbank-like structure of the ECB and the desire of its French president, Jean-Claude Trichet, to demonstrate that he was as Teutonic an inflation fighter as any German.[20]

The United States had not experienced hyperinflation in the 1920s, nor at any other time for that matter, but this did not prevent over-wrought commentators from warning that Weimar was right around the corner.[21] The lesson from the 1930s—that when the economy is in near-depression conditions with interest rates at zero and ample excess capacity, the central bank can expand its balance sheet without igniting inflation—was lost from view. Sophisticated central bankers such as Chairman Bernanke clearly knew better, but there is no doubt that they were influenced by the criticism. The more hysterical the commentary, the more loudly the Congress accused the Fed of debasing the currency. The more Fed governors then feared for their independence. This rendered them anxious to start shrinking the Fed's balance sheet toward normal levels before there was anything resembling a normal economy.

This criticism was more intense to the extent that unconventional policies had gotten central bankers into places they didn't belong, like the market for mortgage-backed securities (Cecchetti 2009). The longer the Fed continued purchasing mortgage-backed securities—and it continued into 2014—the more the institution's critics complained that policy was setting the stage for another housing bubble and another crash. This, of course, was the same preoccupation with moral hazard that had contributed to the disastrous decision not to rescue Lehman Brothers. In the case of the ECB, of course, the moral-hazard worry centered not on the markets but on the politicians. For the central bank to do more to support growth would just relieve the pressure on governments, allowing reforms to lag and risks to accumulate. The ECB allowed itself to be backed into a corner where it was the enforcer of fiscal consolidation and structural reform. And in its role as enforcer, economic growth became the enemy.

In the case of fiscal policy, the argument for continued stimulus was weakened by its failure to deliver everything promised, whether because politicians were prone to overpromising or because the shock to the economy was even worse than understood at the time.[22] There was the failure to distinguish how bad conditions were from how much worse they would have been without the policy. There was the failure to distinguish the need for medium-term consolidation from the need for public support for spending in the short term. There was the failure to distinguish the need for fiscal consolidation in countries with gaping deficits and debts, like Greece, from the situation of countries with the space to do more, like Germany. Thus, a range of factors came together. The one thing they had in common was failure.

Inevitably, failures like these have multiple causes. There was the dominance of ideology and politics over economics analysis. There was the failure of economists to effectively make the case for better policies. There was the tendency of economists to forget as many lessons of the 1930s as they remembered. But the most powerful factor in this premature decision to abandon policies that would have done more to support the economy when the economy still needed support was surely that policymakers had prevented the worst. They had avoided another Great Depression. They could declare the emergency over. They could therefore heed the call for an early return to normal policies. The irony is that their very success in preventing a 1930s-like economic collapse led to their failure to support a more vigorous recovery.

And what was true of macroeconomic policy was also true of financial reform. In the United States, the Great Depression led to the Glass-Steagall Act separating commercial from investment banking. It led to the adoption of federal deposit insurance. It led to the creation of the Securities and Exchange Commission to oversee the operation of securities markets, putting paid to the myth of market self-regulation. There were calls now for a new Glass-Steagall, the earlier act having been laid to rest in 1999, but there was nothing remotely resembling such far-reaching regulatory reform.

The Dodd-Frank Wall Street Reform and Consumer Protection Act of 2010 contained some modestly useful measures, from the Volcker Rule limiting speculative trading by financial institutions to the creation of a Consumer Financial Products Bureau. But the big banks were not broken up. Rhetoric to the contrary, little was done about the problem of too big to fail (Gormley, Johnson, and Rhee 2015). There was nothing approaching the thorough-going redrawing of the financial landscape that resulted from Glass-Steagall's sharp separation of commercial banking, securities underwriting, and insurance services.[23]

The fundamental explanation for the difference is again the success of policymakers in preventing the worst. In the 1930s, the depth of the Depression and the collapse of banks and financial markets wholly discredited the prevailing regime. This time depression and financial collapse were avoided, if barely. This fostered the belief that the flaws of the prevailing system were less. It weakened the argument for radical action, took the wind out of the reformers' sails, allowed the banks to regroup, and allowed petty disagreements among politicians to slow the reform effort. Success thus became the mother of failure.

To be clear, the argument is *not* that it would have been better to allow the big banks to collapse in late 2008 and early 2009. The consequences for output and employment would have been devastating. Avoiding those devastating consequences and limiting unemployment to 10 percent was a considerable achievement, under the circumstances. But it was an achievement with unintended consequences.

The same is true of Europe's failure to embark on more far-reaching financial reform. This reflected the difficulty of decision making in a European Union of 27 countries. But it also reflected the fact that the EU did just enough to hold its monetary union together. Through emergency loans and the creation of an ECB facility to buy the bonds of troubled governments, it did just enough to prevent the euro system from falling apart. This success in turn limited the urgency of proceeding with more far-reaching reform, from across-the-board debt write-downs to creation of a banking union with a single supervisor for all of Europe's banks and a mechanism for directly recapitalizing troubled financial institutions.

Thus, the very success with which policymakers limited the damage from the worst financial crisis in 80 years means that we are likely to see another such crisis in considerably less than 80 years.

This chapter would be incomplete if it didn't address more about Europe and the euro, given how the euro crisis became the second leg of the global financial crisis. The decision to create the euro in 1999 was one of the greatest economic policy blunders of the twentieth century. (A fitting way, some would say, to bring a century of great economic policy blunders to a close.) In this case, unlike the 2008 crisis, some of us like to think—to echo Queen Elizabeth—that we saw it coming: I'm fond of citing my own 1993 article in which I warned of the dangers of creating a monetary union without a banking union, not that this much affected the course of events (Eichengreen 1993).

This decision to go ahead with the euro is another example of the misuses of history—in this case, of the ability of policymakers to cherry-pick their historical analogies. They argued that financial instability and even World War II, indirectly, had been caused by the competitive devaluations of the 1930s, and not by the rigid gold standard system that preceded them, implying that the risk in the 1990s was competitive devaluations rather than the premature creation of a new gold-standard-like system. John F. Kennedy, when contemplating how to respond to the Cuban Missile crisis, considered a range of historical analogies, from Pearl Harbor to the 1948–1949 Berlin Blockade and the 1956 Suez Crisis, and tested them for fitness to the situation at hand. Exceptionally, he had historians like Arthur Schlesinger in his kitchen cabinet (much as Barack Obama had Christina Romer). Harry Truman, who relied only on the analogy with Munich, did not. He had one analogy and pushed it for all it was worth. So too did the architects of the Maastricht Treaty.

The analogy between the gold standard and the euro system became clearer with the onset of the euro crisis, triggered by revelations about Greece's debt and deficits in late 2009. Just as the gold standard prevented national governments and monetary authorities from responding in the 1930s in stabilizing ways, it now became clear that the euro system posed similar obstacles.[24] That earlier conflict had been resolved by abandoning the gold standard, leading many observers to predict that this one would be similarly resolved by abandoning the euro.[25]

This, it turned out, was another misreading of history. In the 1930s, when governments abandoned the gold standard, international trade and lending had already all but collapsed. This time, in contrast, European countries did just enough to avoid that fate. Hence the euro had to be defended in order to preserve the single-market and intra-European trade and payments. In the 1930s, political solidarity was another early casualty of the Depression (Clavin 2010). Notwithstanding the strains of the crisis, governments this time continued to consult and collaborate. All complaints about the European Union notwithstanding, 60 years of European integration fostered a degree of political solidarity considerably greater than that of the 1930s. EU countries in a strong economic and financial position provided loans to their weak European partners. Those loans could have been larger, but they were large by the standards of the 1930s (Accominotti and Eichengreen, forthcoming).

Here, then, is another case where the history of the 1930s was an imperfect guide to policy outcomes. Where the earlier crisis led to the collapse of the gold standard, the recent one has not led to the collapse of the eurozone. At least not yet.

Notes

This chapter draws on my book *Hall of Mirrors: The Great Depression, the Great Recession, and the Uses—and Misuses—of History* (Eichengreen 2015a). The informal and personal tone of this chapter consciously reflects the lecture format for which it was prepared.

1. There is by now an abundant literature by foreign policy specialists making this point. See, for example, Eichengreen (2012), Kyong (1965), Lawrence (2014), May (1973), Neustadt and May (1986), and Shinko (1994).
2. For anticipations of the fact, see Bernanke (2001) and Romer (1992).
3. On psychological biases in general, there is Kahneman (2011).
4. That Friedman and Schwartz in particular had said relatively little about the onset of the Depression was a subtext of Peter Temin's influential book (1976). One important contribution that did discuss the run-up to the Depression at length was that of Temin's MIT colleague Charles Kindleberger (1973). Another noteworthy if only partially successful attempt to develop this aspect of the story is Bernstein (1989).
5. There were rare exceptions, to be sure; see, for example, White (1984).
6. For an attempt to do so after the fact, see Accomminotti and Eichengreen (2016).
7. An early recognition of the point as it applies to the recent crisis is Kohn (2009).
8. See Bernanke (2010) and associated discussion as cited in Pazzanghera (2010). See also the discussion in Geithner (2014).
9. For perspectives on the Lehman Brothers story, see Financial Crisis Inquiry Commission (2011), MacDonald and Robinson (2010), and Sorkin (2010).
10. For details on this crisis, see Kennedy (1973) and Wicker (1996).

11. This was the emphasis of Friedman and Schwartz's influential *Monetary History* (1963).
12. Although it did own an online bank, Lehman Brothers Bank FSB offered community banking services in Delaware, not that this played a key role in the parent institution's failure.
13. Former AIG CEO Maurice ("Hank") Greenberg eventually filed a lawsuit against the federal government disputing the terms of the bailout. At the time of writing, closing arguments were still pending; see Milford and Zajac (2015).
14. As described in the chapter of the same title in Brown (2010).
15. The literature on the impact of these policies is large and characterized by controversy. Among the definitive studies in my view are Feyrer and Sacerdote (2011), Joyce et al. (2011), Krishnamurthy and Vissing-Jorgensen (2011), Mian and Sufi (2012), and Pesaran and Smith (2012).
16. For the current recovery in historical perspective, see Reinhart and Rogoff (2014).
17. Estimates of such impacts differ, of course. A dispassionate analysis, if there is such a thing, is Whalen (2015). The best European equivalent of which I am aware is Barrell, Holland, and Hurst (2012).
18. The literature on fiscal consolidation in Europe is controversial, to put an understated gloss on the point. A meta-analysis of the literature can be found in Gechert, Hughes-Hallett, and Rannenberg (2015).
19. A retrospective analysis with whose conclusions I broadly concur is Rosengren (2015).
20. On Trichet and ECB policy, see Irwin (2015).
21. See the letter from 24 eminent economists published in the *Wall Street Journal* (2010).
22. This is another context in which we are now likely to write the history of the 1920s differently having lived through our own crisis and discovered how difficult it is to track the development of contemporaneous conditions in real time; we are thus likely to better appreciate how contemporaries similarly lacked adequate information on how quickly the economy was in fact contracting in the final months of 1929.
23. A more systematic comparison of financial reform following the two crises is Eichengreen (2015b).
24. A good scholarly analysis is O'Rourke and Taylor (2013).
25. See, for example, O'Brien (2013).

References

Accomminotti, Olivier, and Barry Eichengreen. 2016. "The Mother of All Sudden Stops: Capital Flows and Reversals in Europe, 1919–1932." *Economic History Society* 69(2): 469–492.

Barber, William. 1985. *From New Era to New Deal: Herbert Hoover, the Economists and American Economic Policy 1921–1933*. Cambridge, MA: Cambridge University Press.

Barrell, Ray, Dawn Holland, and Ian Hurst. 2013. "Fiscal Multipliers and Prospects for Consolidation." *OECD Journal of Economic Studies* 2012(1): 71–102.

Bastasin, Carlo. 2015. *Saving Europe*. 2nd ed. Washington, DC: Brookings Institution.

Bernanke, Ben. 2001. *Essays on the Great Depression*. Princeton, NJ: Princeton University Press.

———. 2010. "Causes of the Recent Financial and Economic Crisis." Testimony before the Financial Crisis Inquiry Commission. Washington, DC, September 2.

Bernstein, Michael. 1989. *The Great Depression: Delayed Recovery and Economic Change in America, 1929–1939*. Cambridge, MA: Cambridge University Press.

Brown, Gordon. 2010. *Beyond the Crash: Overcoming the First Crisis of Globalization*. New York: Free Press.

Cecchetti, Steven. 2009. "Crisis and Responses: The Federal Reserve in the Early Stages of the Financial Crisis." *Journal of Economic Perspectives* 23(1): 51–75.

Clavin, Patricia. 2010. *The Great Depression in Europe 1929–1939*. London: Palgrave Macmillan.

Eichengreen, Barry. 1993. "European Monetary Unification." *Journal of Economic Literature* 31(3): 1321–1357.

———. 2012. "Economic History and Economic Policy." *Journal of Economic History* 72(2): 289–307.

———. 2015a. *Hall of Mirrors: The Great Depression, the Great Recession, and the Uses—and Misuses—of History*. New York: Oxford University Press.

———. 2015b. "Time to Get Serious about Financial Reform." *Prospect*, January 22. https://www.prospectmagazine.co.uk/magazine/time-to-get-serious-about-bank-reform (accessed April 27, 2017).

Feyrer, James, and Bruce Sacerdote. 2011. "Did the Stimulus Stimulate? Real Time Estimates of the Effects of the American Recovery and Reinvestment Act." NBER Working Paper No. 16759. Cambridge, MA: National Bureau of Economic Research.

Financial Crisis Inquiry Commission. 2011. *Final Report of the National Commission on the Causes of the Financial and Economic Crisis in the United States*. Washington, DC: U.S. Government Printing Office. http://www.gpo.gov/fdsys/pkg/GPO-FCIC/pdf/GPO-FCIC.pdf (accessed April 27, 2017).

Friedman, Milton, and Anna Schwartz. 1963. *A Monetary History of the United States, 1867-1960*. Princeton, NJ: Princeton University Press for the National Bureau of Economic Research.

Gechert, Sebastian, Andrew Hughes-Hallett, and Ansgar Rannenberg. 2015.

"Fiscal Multipliers in Downturns and the Effects of Eurozone Consolidation." *CEPR Policy Insights* 79: 1–6.

Geithner, Timothy. 2014. *Stress Test: Reflections on Financial Crises*. New York: Crown.

Gormley, Todd, Simon Johnson, and Changyong Rhee. 2015. "Ending 'Too Big to Fail': Government Promises versus Investor Perceptions." *Review of Finance* 19(2): 491–518.

Igan, Deniz, and Prachi Mishra. 2011. "Three's Company: Wall Street, Capitol Hill and K Street." IMF Working Paper. Washington, DC: International Monetary Fund.

Igan, Deniz, Prachi Mishra, and Thierry Tressel. 2011. "A Fistful of Dollars: Lobbying and the Financial Crisis." In *NBER Macroeconomics Annual, Vol 26*, Daron Acemoglu and Michael Woodford, eds. Chicago: University of Chicago Press, pp. 195–230.

Irwin, Neil. 2013. *The Alchemists: Three Central Bankers and a World on Fire*. New York: Penguin.

Joyce, Michael, Anna Lasaosa, Ibrahim Stevens, and Matthew Tong. 2011. "The Financial Market Impact of Quantitative Easing in the United Kingdom." Unpublished manuscript. Bank of England: London.

Kahneman, Daniel. 2011. *Thinking, Fast and Slow*. New York: Farrar, Strauss, and Giroux.

Kennedy, Susan Estabrook. 1973. *The Banking Crisis of 1933*. Lexington, KY: University Press of Kentucky.

Kindleberger, Charles. 1973. *The World in Depression, 1929–1939*. Berkeley: University of California Press.

Kohn, Donald. 2009. "Monetary Policy and Asset Prices Revisited." *Cato Journal* 29(1): 31–44.

Krishnamurthy, Arvind, and Annette Vissing-Jorgensen. 2011. "The Effects of Quantitative Easing on Interest Rates: Channels and Implications for Policy." *Brookings Papers on Economic Activity* Fall: 215–265.

Kyong, Yuen Foong. 1965. *Analogies at War: Korea, Munich, Dien Bien Phu and the Vietnam Decisions of 1965*. Princeton: Princeton University Press.

Lawrence, Paul Atwood. 2014. "Foreign Policy by Analogy: U.S. Decision Making and the Uses of the Vietnam War." Unpublished manuscript, University of Texas at Austin.

MacDonald, Lawrence, and Patrick Robinson. 2010. *A Colossal Failure of Common Sense: The Inside Story of the Collapse of Lehman Brothers*. New York: Crown Business.

May, Ernest. 1973. *"Lessons" from the Past*. New York: Oxford University Press.

Mian, Atif, and Amir Sufi. 2012. "The Effects of Fiscal Stimulus: Evidence from the 2009 'Cash for Clunkers' Program." *Quarterly Journal of Economics* 127(3): 1007–1042.

Mian, Atif, Amir Sufi, and Francesco Trebbi. 2010. "The Political Economy of the U.S. Mortgage Default Crisis." *American Economic Review* 100(5): 1967–1998.

Milford, Phil, and Andrew Zajac. 2015. "Closing Arguments in Greenberg's Suit Against Bailout Set from April 22." *Insurance Journal*, March 24. http://www.insurancejournal.com/news/national/2015/03/24/361846.htm (accessed April 27, 2017).

Neustadt, Richard and Ernest May. 1986. *Thinking in Time: The Uses of History for Decision Makers*. New York: Free Press.

O'Brien, Matthew. 2013. "Why the Euro Is Doomed in Four Steps—It's the Gold Standard Minus the Shiny Rocks." *Atlantic*, March 30. http://www.theatlantic.com/business/archive/2013/03/why-the-euro-is-doomed-in-4-steps/274470/ (accessed April 28, 2017).

Omer, Haim, and Nahman Alon. 1994. "The Continuity Principle: A Unified Approach to Disaster and Trauma." *American Journal of Community Psychology* 22(2): 273–287.

O'Rourke, Kevin, and Alan Taylor. 2013. "Cross of Euros." *Journal of Economic Perspectives* 27(3): 167–191.

Patomaki, Heikki. 2009. "Neoliberalism and the Global Financial Crisis." *New Political Science* 31(4): 431–443.

Pazzanghera, Jim. 2010. "Bernanke Says Fed Had to Let Lehman Fail." *Los Angeles Times*, September 3. http://articles.latimes.com/2010/sep/03/business/la-fi-crisis-bernanke-20100903 (accessed April 28, 2017).

Pesaran, Hashem, and Ron Smith. 2012. "Counterfactual Analysis in Macroeconomics: An Empirical Investigation into the Effects of Quantitative Easing." IZA Discussion Paper No. 6618. Bonn: IZA.

Pierce, Andrew. 2008. "The Queen Asks Why No One Saw the Credit Crunch Coming?" *Telegraph*, November 5. http://www.telegraph.co.uk/news/uknews/theroyalfamily/3386353/The-Queen-asks-why-no-one-saw-the-credit-crunch-coming.html (accessed April 28, 2017).

Rajan, Raghuram. 2005. "Has Financial Development Made the World Riskier?" In *The Greenspan Era: Lessons for the Future*. Federal Reserve Bank of Kansas City. Kansas City: Federal Reserve Bank of Kansas City, pp. 313–369.

Reinhart, Carmen, and Kenneth Rogoff. 2014. "Recovery from Financial Crises: Evidence from 100 Episodes." *American Economic Review: Papers and Proceedings* 104(5): 50–55.

Romer, Christina. 1992. "What Ended the Great Depression?" *Journal of Economic History* 52(4): 957–984.

Rosengren, Eric. 2015. "Lessons from the U.S. Experience with Quantitative Easing." Speech to the Peterson Institute/Moody's Joint Event, held in Frankfurt, Germany, February 5. http://www.bostonfed.org/news/press/2015/pr020515.htm.

Shinko, Keith. 1994. "Metaphors and Foreign Policy Decision Making." *Political Psychology* 15(4): 655–671.

Sorkin, Andrew Ross. 2010. *Too Big to Fail: The Story of How Wall Street and Washington Fought to Save the Financial System—and Themselves*. New York: Penguin.

Suarez, Sandra, and Robin Kolodny. 2011. "Paving the Road to 'Too Big to Fail': Business Interests and the Politics of Financial Deregulation in the U.S." *Politics & Society* 39(1): 74–102.

Telegraph. 2009. "Queen Told How Economists Missed Financial Crisis." July 26. http://www.telegraph.co.uk/news/uknews/theroyalfamily/5912697/Queen-told-how-economists-missed-financial-crisis.html (accessed April 27, 2017).

Temin, Peter. 1976. *Did Monetary Forces Cause the Great Depression?* New York: Norton.

Vickers, Raymond. 2011. *Panic in the Loop: Chicago's Banking Crisis of 1932*. Lanham, MD: Lexington Books.

Wall Street Journal. 2010. "Open Letter to Ben Bernanke." *Economics* (blog), *Wall Street Journal* November 15. http://blogs.wsj.com/economics/2010/11/15/open-letter-to-ben-bernanke and archived at http://economics21.org/commentary/e21s-open-letter-ben-bernanke (accessed April 27, 2017).

Whalen, Charles. 2015. "The Fiscal Multiplier and Economic Policy Analysis in the United States." Working Paper No. 2015-02. Washington, DC: Congressional Budget Office.

White, Eugene. 1984. "Banking Innovation in the 1920s: The Growth of National Banks' Financial Services." *Business and Economic History* 13: 92–104.

Wicker, Elmus. 1996. *The Banking Panics of the Great Depression*. Cambridge, MA: Cambridge University Press.

3

The Great Recession and Lessons for Policymaking

Gary Burtless
Brookings Institution

This chapter addresses a straightforward question: What policy lessons can we draw from the Great Recession? At the time of this writing in late 2014, the lessons have more academic than practical interest to policymakers in Washington. Most decision-makers are more concerned about the next election than they are about warnings from an experience that is unlikely to soon be repeated. However, examining the experience may be useful when considering policies to prevent or manage a future downturn.

The Great Recession produced the worst economic slump since the Great Depression. Compared with other post–World War II recessions, the one in 2008–2009 was particularly severe and the recovery from it unusually sluggish. This is clear from a glance at job market statistics: the spike in the unemployment rate—5.5 percentage points between the first half of 2007 and October 2009—was the biggest the country experienced in the postwar era; the persistence of high joblessness was uncommonly severe; and the unemployment rate remained above 8 percent for 43 consecutive months. The only postwar rival in terms of severity was the recession during the Reagan administration, which began in the summer of 1981. The unemployment rate in the 1980s remained above 8 percent for only 27 consecutive months.

The consequences of the Great Recession for job losers and new job entrants were unusually harsh. Over the entire postwar era before the Great Recession, the median duration of unemployment reached a peak of just 12.3 weeks, which occurred in May 1983 during the recovery from the Reagan recession. In the recent slump, the median duration of unemployment reached a peak more than twice as high, 25 weeks, and it remained above 13 weeks for an astonishing 67 consecutive months. The BLS employment report for November 2014 showed that the median unemployment duration for that month fell below 13 weeks for the first time since March 2009.

As painful as it was, however, the Great Recession was not remotely as severe as the Great Depression, which was "great" in its depth and duration. The peak unemployment rate in the 1930s was 25 percent, compared to just 10 percent during and after the Great Recession. Between the fall of 1929 and the spring of 1933, the U.S. economy shrank for 43 consecutive months, whereas in the recent recession the economy shrank for just 18 months. At the end of the 1929–1933 downturn, real GDP per person was about 29 percent smaller than it was just before the Depression began (Figure 3.1), compared to about 5 percent between 2007 and 2009. In the Great Depression, per capita GDP did not return to its pre-Depression level until 1937, a span of eight years; it

Figure 3.1 U.S. Gross Domestic Product per Person in the Great Depression and Great Recession

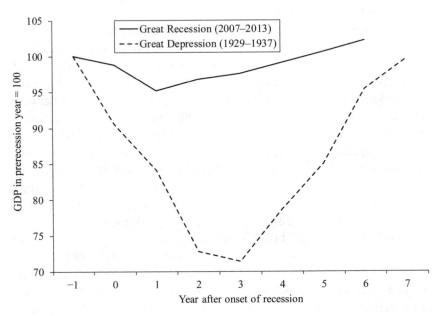

SOURCE: Dept. of Commerce, Bureau of Economic Analysis, National Income and Product Accounts.

took a little less than five years after the Great Recession for per capita GDP to surpass its prerecession peak.

The Great Depression saw personal consumption per person fall 21 percent below its pre-Depression level. In the worst year of the Depression, the typical American consumed about one-fifth fewer goods and services than in the last pre-Depression year. In the Great Recession, per capita real consumption fell just 4 percent. Whatever the shortcomings of macroeconomic policymaking in recent years, the fact is that the U.S. economy performed far better between 2007 and 2014 than it did in the decade that began in 1929. U.S. macro policies in the recent downturn also delivered better results than the ones devised by policymakers in most other rich countries. Nonetheless, "It could have been worse" is not a winning political slogan, a fact emphatically confirmed by U.S. voters in the three elections after the recovery began. "It could have been worse" is, however, a fair assessment of fiscal policymaking over the past seven years. The question this chapter poses is, "How could it have been better?"

BACKGROUND

The federal government did not stand still in the face of the severe contraction in late 2008. It dealt promptly with the financial crisis that triggered the downturn. In fact, the rescue of ailing financial institutions was mostly accomplished within a year after the worst phase of the crisis. My critique focuses mostly on fiscal rather than monetary policy. Fiscal policy is where U.S. policymakers, as well as those in much of the industrialized world, fell furthest below the mark. Still, it is worth remembering that an emergency law passed by Congress in October 2008 and an extraordinary series of steps by the Federal Reserve Board (Fed) in 2008 and early 2009 were needed to keep the U.S. financial system functioning.

Monetary Policy

Already worried by signs of financial market instability, the Fed began to cut short-term interest rates in the summer of 2007, when the economy was still growing and the stock market climbing. By May 2008, the central bank reduced its policy interest rate from 5.25 percent to 2.0 percent. On September 15, 2008, Lehman Brothers, the nation's fourth-largest investment bank, declared bankruptcy. The bank's collapse triggered a worldwide panic and started the worst phase of the financial crisis. In response, the Federal Reserve lowered its policy interest rate still further. By the end of 2008 the federal funds rate, which is the interest rate banks use to make overnight loans to one another, was cut to its lowest level of the modern era. In the 16 months after August 2007, the Fed cut its benchmark short-term rate by 5.1 points, to essentially zero.

The Fed also extended extraordinary credits to both banks and non-bank institutions in exchange for high-quality collateral. This emergency measure was needed to keep credit flowing in markets where ordinary lending had practically ceased. Without this step many solvent financial and nonfinancial companies would have been forced to either enter bankruptcy or sharply curtail their normal operations. Many firms would have been cut off from routine short-term borrowing. By keeping credit flowing in the middle of a panic, the Fed kept the financial market crisis from metastasizing into something much worse. The real economy took a beating, but if credit markets had completely seized up, the damage could have been catastrophic. Providing liquidity in a crisis is a classic role of a well-functioning central bank.

When the Fed pushed its policy interest rate to zero in late 2008, it exhausted the standard measures used by central banks to encourage borrowing and spur growth. With safe, short-term interest rates close to zero, the Fed either had to watch from the sidelines or take unconventional steps to encourage lending and borrowing. One of the main tools it used after late 2008 was quantitative easing. This strategy involves the Fed's purchase of longer-term Treasury securities than it ordinarily holds, as well as purchases of private market securities, including mortgage-backed securities. These purchases can potentially reduce market interest rates on intermediate- and longer-term private securities. Through the fall of 2014 the Fed purchased $1.6 trillion in Treasury bonds and $1.7 trillion in mortgage-backed securities in three different sequences, all in an effort to push down intermediate- and long-term interest rates.

The logic behind this strategy is that by reducing longer-term interest rates the Fed might encourage some consumers and firms who otherwise would not have borrowed funds to do so. Their borrowing can in turn give a boost to business investment, new home building, and purchases of consumer durable goods, such as cars. Experts on monetary policy, consumer spending, and business investment have not reached a consensus on whether this policy has worked. What seems clear is that the Fed was pushed to adopt unconventional policies because Congress failed to adopt a fiscal policy that is appropriate when the economy is operating far below its potential and when short-term interest rates on safe securities are close to zero.

Fiscal Policy

With prodding from two presidents, Congress authorized a series of fiscal policy measures to boost consumer incomes, induce businesses to expand investment, and protect state-level spending on health, education, and public infrastructure. Most of the special government measures in response to the Great Recession were familiar ones: Temporary tax reductions to boost consumer incomes and encourage business investment; extensions of unemployment benefits and liberalization of other government transfer programs, including food stamps and social assistance; and increased federal appropriations for new government investment in buildings, roads, and science and technology projects. The special fiscal measures included some unusual measures as well. For the first time, the federal government paid for generous insurance subsidies for laid-off workers who lost health insurance when they lost their jobs. It also provided unusually liberal grants to state governments to encourage them to maintain or increase spending on core state obligations, such as K–12 education and health care for the indigent. President Obama used funds authorized under the Troubled Asset Relief Program (TARP) to finance emergency lending and fast-track bankruptcy funding to preserve General Motors, Chrysler, and many auto supply companies. A small share of emergency stimulus appropriations was used to fund or provide loans to projects aimed at improving energy efficiency and reducing carbon emissions.

It should be emphasized that an overwhelming percentage of stimulus dollars was spent on programs that would have been familiar to policymakers and economists in every recession since the early 1960s. This is true whether the administration was Democratic or Republican, liberal or conservative. This is also true whether Congress was controlled by Democrats or Republicans, liberals or conservatives. The emphasis and overall scale of stimulus programs have differed depending on the political leanings of the party in control of Congress and the White House. However, Republican and conservative critics of recent fiscal policy are kidding themselves (and voters) when they claim to be horrified by the actual contents and additions to the deficit connected with the stimulus. Republicans were in control of either the White House or Congress (or both) in recessions in the mid-1970s, in the early 1980s, in 2001–2003, and in 2008. Many elements of the stimulus program adopted in 2009 and 2010 were also present in the fiscal policies adopted in those recessions—notably, big tax cuts, generous extensions of unemployment benefits, and extra outlays on public capital investment. In 2008–2009 the scale and speed of the additions to peacetime deficits were unprecedented, to be sure. But that is because after Lehman Brothers entered bankruptcy the nation faced the frightening prospect of financial market collapse. Even though the risk was reduced to a manageable level by spring 2009, the effects of the financial crisis on the real economy were obvious, severe, and still growing well into 2010.

The fact that most postwar administrations and Congresses would have pursued the same or a similar set of stimulus policies has not altered a basic reality. The popular political reaction to some of the best-known policies has been intensely hostile. In particular, the financial rescue of the nation's biggest banks and automakers inspired widespread public indignation. The federal bailout of big banks appeared to reward firms whose imprudent, even reckless behavior helped to create the crisis. Many voters may have incorrectly believed that an overwhelming share of public funds used to restore the economy was spent on bailouts for big banks and automakers. In fact, far more resources were devoted to temporary tax cuts for middle-income families, emergency relief for laid-off workers and their families, and generous grants to state and local governments. The confusion is understandable. After Democrats gained control of both the White House and Congress in January 2009, Republican opponents of fiscal stimulus were unrelenting in their criticism of selected components of the countercyclical program. Many liberal Democrats joined Republicans in fiercely criticizing the aid extended to big financial institutions. Voters may have wrongly inferred that the controversial parts of the stimulus package consumed an out-sized share of the program's cost.

The extreme and unbending hostility of political opponents to the fiscal measures has had practical consequences. First, fierce opposition from conservatives, including a handful of fiscally conservative Democrats, deterred the administration from proposing a stimulus package that was adequate given the magnitude of the shock to the economy. This opposition reduced the size of the stimulus the administration could persuade Congress to pass. Second, Republican gains in the House of Representatives in the 2010 election led to an unwinding of fiscal stimulus long before the economy had recovered from the recession. This was the single worst error in macroeconomic policymaking following the financial crisis in fall 2008. The fact that policymakers in other rich countries made even worse errors in both fiscal and monetary policy does not excuse the fiscal policy errors of U.S. decision makers. For reasons that may seem mysterious to future economic historians, members of Congress, opinion leaders, and ultimately voters decided that the "crisis" of rising public debt represented a more pressing challenge to the nation than soaring long-term unemployment and the under-utilization of U.S. productive capacity. There is no evidence that people who buy and sell securities ever shared the view that the United States was accumulating an unsustainable debt burden. The government was able to sell indexed and unindexed short- and long-term Treasury at historically low interest rates throughout the crisis and its aftermath. Nonetheless, the fear of rising national debt pushed opinion leaders to urge Congress to adopt a more conservative fiscal policy after 2009 than would have seemed appropriate based on the historical record from 1929 to 2007.

Fortunately, the private economy began to grow again in late 2009, and between 2010 and 2014, private sector payrolls grew faster than 200,000 a month. Unfortunately, the downturn was severe, and the growing working-age population needs 75,000 net new jobs every month just to keep the unemployment rate from rising. For the past four years, public sector spending and hiring have done little to speed the pace of recovery. In fact, in the three years through 2013, a drop in public employee payrolls offset about 6 percent of the job gains generated in the private sector. Reductions in public payrolls and also in govern-

ment consumption and investment created unnecessary headwinds for
a weak recovery.

Sharp Downturn, Weak Recovery

The labor market effects of the 2008–2009 recession were severe
compared with those of any other postwar recession. More disturbingly,
the recovery was unusually slow. It is enlightening to compare the recent
recession with the one that began in 1981, which was the worst postwar
downturn before the Great Recession. Figure 3.2 shows the trend in the
unemployment rate before and after the onset of the two recessions. The
unemployment rate in each case is measured relative to the rate at the
business cycle peak as designated by the National Bureau of Economic
Research.[1] The business cycle peak is indicated on the horizontal axis
by "0" and other months by the number of months before or after the
business cycle peak. The chart tracks the difference between the unem-

Figure 3.2 Change in Unemployment Rate in Two Postwar Recessions

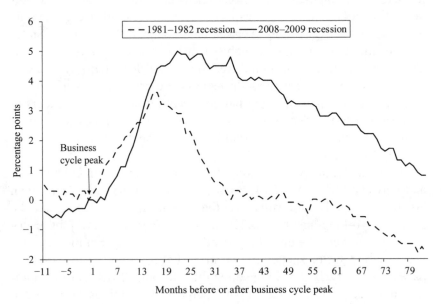

SOURCE: U.S. Bureau of Labor Statistics.

ployment rate in the indicated month and the rate at the business cycle peak. The estimates show unemployment changes in the year before the recession began up through the eighty-second month after the previous business cycle peak. The 1981–1982 recession initially saw a steeper rise in the unemployment rate. Slightly more than a year after the onset of the recession, however, the increase in joblessness was greater in the Great Recession, and the unemployment rate continued to rise for 22 months rather than just 16. Crucially, the decline in joblessness has been much slower in the most recent business cycle. By the thirty-fifth month, unemployment was back to its prerecession level in the 1981–1982 downturn but was still 4.8 percentage points higher than the prerecession level in the Great Recession. By the eighty-second month after the beginning of the Great Recession, unemployment was still 0.8 percentage points higher than it was when the recession began. At the comparable point after the Reagan recession, the jobless rate was 1.6 points below where it was when the recession began.

Figure 3.3 shows the same kind of comparison for the decline and recovery of payroll employment in the two recessions. The drop in employment was initially more severe in the 1981–1982 recession, but by the thirteenth month after the downturn began the percentage drop in payroll employment was greater in the Great Recession. In the eighteenth month after the onset of the 1981–1982 recession, employment began to recover. Employment did not begin to climb in the Great Recession until the twenty-eighth month after the business cycle peak in late 2007. By the eighty-second month after the beginning of the recession, payroll employment in the 1981–1982 recession was 14.6 percent above its prerecession peak. In the same month of the most recent business cycle, employment was only 0.8 percentage points above its prerecession peak. Not only were the labor market effects of the recent recession deeper than those of any other postwar recession, they have also lingered much longer.

Why Was the Recovery So Weak?

The key event that triggered the steep slide in the 2008 economy was the near-death experience of the biggest U.S. financial institutions. Their brush with disaster interrupted normal credit flows and, more to the point, made credit-worthy households and businesses worry about

**Figure 3.3 Change in Total Payroll Employment in Two
            Postwar Recessions**

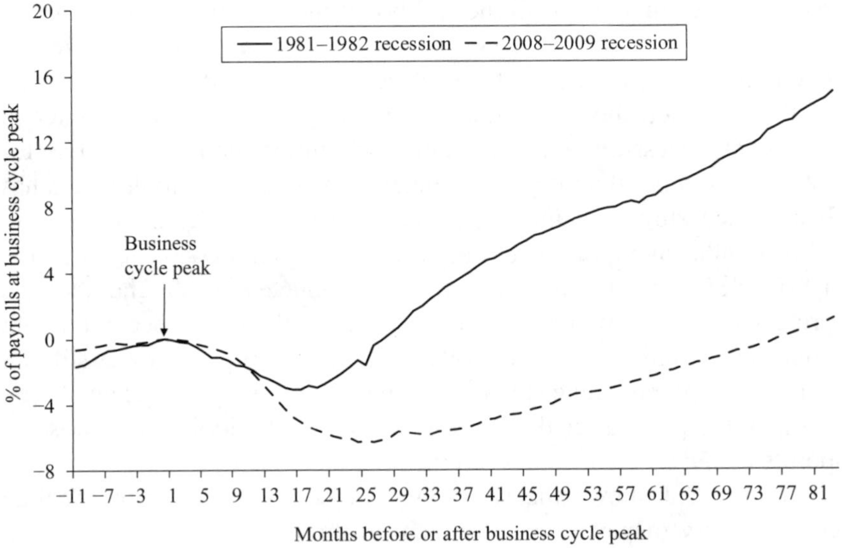

Months before or after business cycle peak

SOURCE: U.S. Bureau of Labor Statistics.

their future access to credit. Investors and businesses fled riskier assets and bid up the prices of the safest assets, particularly U.S. government debt.

The underlying cause of financial institutions' weakness can be traced to the run-up in house and apartment prices followed by the steep slide in many parts of the country. The rise in prices encouraged households to borrow and increase their consumption more than they would have done based on their incomes alone. The accelerating decline in house prices after 2006 wiped out much or all of this extra wealth and simultaneously destroyed the credit-worthiness of a large percentage of households. Between 2007 and 2009 the combined effects of declining real estate and stock market prices erased $19 trillion of household wealth—one-quarter of household net worth at the peak. This drop in wealth would be expected to reduce household consumption by $450 billion a year if we assume, conservatively, that households boost annual consumption by $4 for every $100 increase in their net worth.

If many consumers spend an even larger percentage of their net gains from house price gains, the combined drop in house and stock prices would reduce consumer spending by $750 billion per year.[2]

Figure 3.4 shows the rise and subsequent fall in home prices compared with all other prices in the U.S. economy. Between the late 1990s and 2006, house prices increased by half relative to other prices; by 2012 they lost about six-tenths of that gain. Between 2006 and the end of 2012, they fell one-quarter. Since many homeowners had borrowed heavily either to buy their homes or to convert their capital gains into ready spending money, a large percentage of them ended up with negative equity in their homes. If they also saw their incomes drop as a result of a bad job market, they simultaneously faced the risk of losing possession of their homes.

The surge in house prices between 2003 and 2006 was accompanied by a strong rise in stock prices. Appreciating stock values helped boost

Figure 3.4 Index of Real U.S. House Prices, 1975–2014, Q1

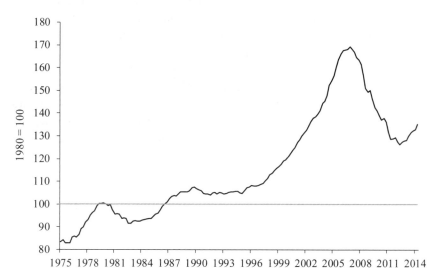

NOTE: Federal Housing Finance Agency index of U.S.-average house price is deflated using the GDP deflator.

SOURCE: Federal Housing Finance Agency and U.S. Department of Commerce, Bureau of Economic Analysis.

consumption among households that owned equities. When equity owners lost faith in U.S. financial institutions and then in the companies that depended on them, stock prices plunged. Equity prices fell about half between the fall of 2007 and the first quarter of 2009. The collapse of stock prices affected the net worth of a different group of households than those suffering sharp losses as a result of the housing collapse. Stockholders tend to be considerably richer on average than the typical homeowner. Nonetheless, wealthy Americans also consume, and their consumption is affected by the value of their wealth holdings.

The best summary measure of American's wealth holdings is the ratio of their household net worth to their disposable income. This ratio reached a peak of 6.5-to-1 in 2006 and then fell back to 5-to-1 in early 2009 (Figure 3.5). The deflation of the house price bubble, the loss of confidence in major financial institutions, and collapsing stock market valuations erased one-quarter of net household wealth. After 2007 consumption was no longer being turbo-charged by soaring household wealth; it was being pushed down by the drop in household net worth.

Most large nonfinancial businesses entered the recession with reasonably strong balance sheets. Except for short-term borrowing needs, many of them did not have a pressing need for credit to maintain their operations. But to persuade a business to invest, the business owner must also be persuaded that there will be a market for the added output that would be produced by new investment. Business managers and owners read the same news stories as the rest of us—after Lehman Brothers' collapse, they faced the chilling prospect of consumer retrenchment.

The drop in home prices extinguished many families' chances for added borrowing. But even families with ample wealth faced the reality that not only was their net worth no longer rising, it was sinking fast. In this environment, households consumed less, businesses sold less, and sensible business managers anticipated that household spending would remain low, erasing the potential payoff from new investment. If a firm is already operating at 30 percent below capacity, why spend funds to expand that capacity? Even with short- and intermediate-term interest rates at historical lows, the attractions of additional investment appeared meager.

The outlook improved when stock prices recovered and home prices began to rise again. Even so, the Federal Reserve's Survey of Consumer Finances suggests that average household net worth for middle- and

Figure 3.5 Ratio of Net Household Wealth to Household Disposable Income, 1974–2014, Q2

SOURCE: Board of Governors of the Federal Reserve System, Financial Accounts of the United States.

lower-income families was lower in late 2014 than it was in the late 1980s.[3] The top wealth holders are undoubtedly much better off today than they were in the aftermath of the Great Recession, but the same is not true of lower-income households whose 2007 wealth consisted mainly of the equity in their homes.

The dismal employment numbers I cite above, combined with appalling wealth losses, may lead some readers to wonder why per capita consumption fell "only" 4 percent from its peak prerecession level to its low point in the Great Recession. One answer is that the U.S. social safety net worked very well in the Great Recession. When we entered the recession, neither the Congress nor the president was interested in dismantling the safety net. In fact, President Obama and the 2009–2010 Congress enacted important and permanent additions to the safety net. Furthermore, Congress and two administrations acted promptly to shore up consumer incomes through a range of temporary tax cuts and enhancements of the safety net.

Even if policymakers do not act to boost the economy in a recession, the nation's permanent tax and transfer system has built-in stabilizers that automatically lessen the income losses suffered by the unemployed. Quantitatively, the biggest single item is federal tax payments, especially payroll and personal and corporate income taxes, which tend to fall faster than private incomes when recessions cause pretax incomes to shrink.

The second-biggest item is unemployment benefits. Experienced workers who lose their jobs through no fault of their own ordinarily qualify for up to six months of Unemployment Insurance benefits. In recessions, benefits can last longer depending on the severity of unemployment in a job loser's state of residence. Although U.S. unemployment benefits are low compared to those available in most other wealthy countries, workers earning the average wage typically qualify for benefits that compensate them for half the loss of their prelayoff earnings.[4] Because the number of laid-off workers qualifying for benefits rises steeply in a recession, the money spent on jobless benefits also increases sharply. In every recession since the late 1950s, Congress has authorized temporary emergency extensions of unemployment benefits, financed with federal funds. It did so again in 2008 and 2009, increasing the maximum duration of unemployment benefits to 99 weeks in states with the highest unemployment rates. In no previous recession had Congress authorized such a lengthy extension of benefits. In addition, Congress financed a temporary increase in weekly unemployment benefit checks, and it reduced the income tax levied on benefits. Between 2007 and 2010, annual outlays on unemployment benefits increased more than 4.5 times, rising from $35 billion to $160 billion.

In addition to temporary improvements in unemployment benefits, the federal government also authorized increases in monthly food stamp allotments, extra funding for state governments' social assistance programs for children, and a doubling of the prerecession budget for training the unemployed and hard-to-employ. Congress also enacted temporary measures to cut household payroll and income tax payments. For example, it increased the Earned Income and Child Tax Credits, and it authorized a temporary payroll tax credit of $400 per worker and $800 per couple in 2009 and 2010, with the credit phased out for upper income families. When the temporary tax cuts ended in 2011, they were replaced by a temporary cut in the Social Security payroll tax of 2 percentage points. Many low- and moderate-income families do not owe income or payroll taxes, and consequently did not benefit under these provisions. For some of these families—in particular, those receiving Social Security and veterans' benefits—the 2009 stimulus bill granted one-time payments in lieu of the tax cuts.

Automatic income stabilization combined with generous temporary measures to shore up household income achieved their intended aim: Household net income fell proportionately far less than the drop in private income. This is illustrated in Figure 3.6, which shows the 2007–2014 trends in gross market income and disposable personal income. Trends in both income series are measured on a per capita basis as a percentage of estimated incomes in the fourth quarter of 2007, the last calendar quarter of the economic expansion that ended in 2007. Incomes in each period are converted into constant purchasing power units using the personal consumption expenditure deflator. The line in the chart

Figure 3.6 Impact of the Great Recession on Pretax Market Income and Disposable Income, 2007Q1–2014Q3

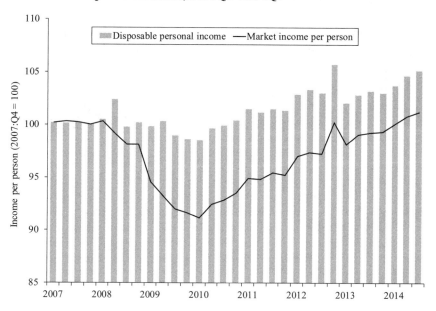

SOURCE: Dept. of Commerce, Bureau of Economic Analysis, National Income and Product Accounts.

shows the trend in pretax market income per person. Market income consists of gross labor compensation to employees, self-employment income of business owners, interest, dividends, rental payments, and other flows of pretax capital income. Per capita market income fell sharply in the recession, declining 8.8 percent by the first quarter of 2010. Spendable income, indicated by the bars in Figure 3.6, fell proportionately much less. Increases in government transfers and reduced personal taxes cushioned households' income loss. In the period with the worst income loss, the first quarter of 2010, disposable income per person was only 1.5 percent below its level at the end of the previous expansion.

Figure 3.7 compares the trend in pretax market income with changes in the level of government transfers per person. The bars in the chart show the level of real government transfers per person, measured as a percentage of transfers per person in the final quarter of 2007. Note

Figure 3.7 Trends in Pretax Market Income and Government Transfer Payments, 2007Q1–2014Q3

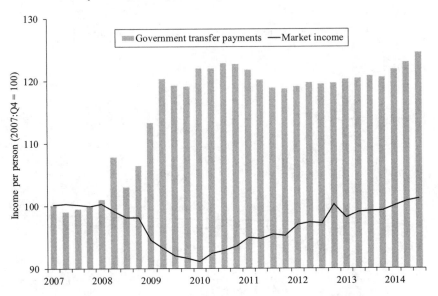

SOURCE: Dept. of Commerce, Bureau of Economic Analysis, National Income and Product Accounts.

the steep increase in transfers starting as early as the second quarter of 2008, when the Bush administration and Congress enacted the first countercyclical stimulus program. By the second quarter of 2009, transfer payments per person were 20 percent higher than in the quarter before the recession began.

Now consider all three components of disposable personal income, shown in Figure 3.8: 1) pretax market income (wages, fringe benefits, self-employment earnings, rent, interest, and dividends); 2) direct tax payments to the government (mainly social insurance and personal income tax payments); and 3) transfer payments received from the government. Measuring each of these variables relative to their levels in the last quarter of 2007, the trend lines in the chart show how per capita amounts changed over the period from 2007 through 2014:Q3. As a result of progressive income taxation and the temporary tax cuts effective over the period 2008–2012, personal tax payments fell, both

Figure 3.8 Components of Real Disposable Personal Income per Person, 2007Q1–2014Q3

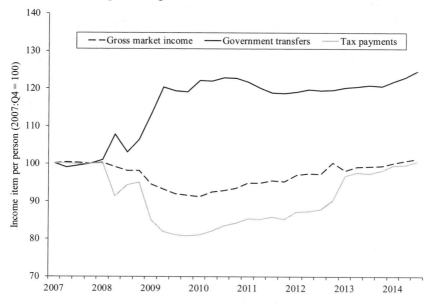

SOURCE: Dept. of Commerce, Bureau of Economic Analysis, National Income and Product Accounts.

absolutely and as a percentage of households' pretax incomes. By the third quarter of 2009, per capita tax payments fell almost 20 percent, about twice the proportional drop in pretax market income. The temporary tax cuts were phased out at the end of 2012, so the trend in tax payments after that year mirrors the trend in pretax market income. As noted above, the increase in real government transfers per person has not yet been phased out. Transfer payments continue to supplement family incomes more than they did before the Great Recession.

In view of the sharp increase in transfer income and the sizable temporary cuts in personal taxes, it should not be surprising that personal consumption fell much less than market income in the Great Recession, a pattern highlighted in Figure 3.9. The line in the figure traces the trend in pretax market income per person. Note that per capita market income fell nearly 9 percent between 2007 and the first quarter of 2010. The bars in the chart show the trend in real consumption expenditures per person, measured as a percent of the personal consumption level in the last quarter before the recession. Even at the worst point in the recession, the second quarter of 2009, personal consumption fell just 4 percent—a larger drop than the one we observed in per capita disposable income (see Figure 3.6). It is, however, far smaller than the drop in pretax market income. The stimulus program combined with automatic stabilizers undoubtedly worked in the sense that they dramatically reduced the decline in spendable incomes. By helping to hold up spendable income, they also lessened the drop in consumer expenditures. Recall that household net worth fell one-quarter while household market incomes fell one-eleventh. It represents a considerable achievement that per capita, real consumption fell only 4 percent below its previous peak in the worst quarter of the Great Recession.

The changes in tax burdens and in government transfers tended to favor low- and middle-income families, especially those with a laid-off worker, over families with higher incomes. The Congressional Budget Office (CBO) publishes periodic analyses of the distribution of federal tax burdens (e.g., CBO [2014]). The analyses distinguish three definitions of income: gross market incomes (including capital gains and an imputation to households of the undistributed income of corporations in which they have ownership share); pretax income (gross market income plus government transfers); and after-tax income (pretax income minus federal taxes, including payroll, income, and excise taxes). The most

Figure 3.9 Trends in Pretax Market Income and Personal Consumption Expenditures per Person, 2007Q1–2014Q3

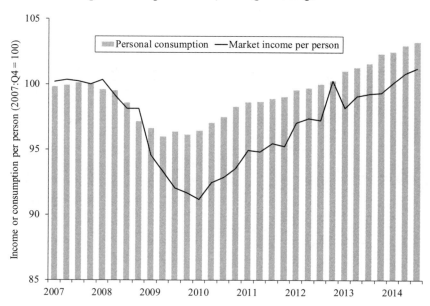

SOURCE: Dept. of Commerce, Bureau of Economic Analysis, National Income and Product Accounts.

recent published CBO data cover the period from 1979 through 2011, and they permit us to determine how incomes under these three definitions differ across the household income distribution and over time. CBO's results for the period 2007–2011 permit us to see how gross market income and after-tax income (including government transfers) changed in different positions of the income distribution. Figure 3.10 shows the 2007–2011 change in pretax market income and after-tax income across the distribution. Households are ranked by the CBO based on their pretax market plus transfer income. Panel A shows percent changes in pretax market incomes; Panel B shows percent changes in after-tax incomes. Results on the left show income changes in the bottom four-fifths of the income distribution; results on the right show changes in the top fifth of the distribution. The latter results are subdivided into results for the 81st–90th income percentile, the 91st–95th

Figure 3.10 Estimates of Changes in Market Income and Posttax, Posttransfer Income by Position in Household Income Distribution, 2007–2011

Panel A: Percent change in market income

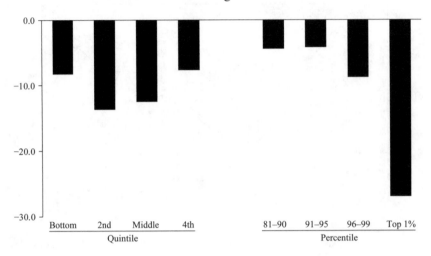

Panel B: Percent change in posttax, posttransfer income

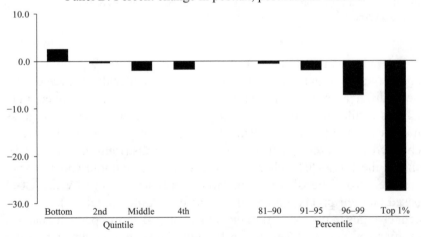

SOURCE: Congressional Budget Office (2014). Income groups are created by ranking households by their pretax income, adjusted for family size. Each fifth of the distribution contains an equal number of people.

percentile, the 96th–99th percentile, and the top 1 percent of pretax income recipients.

The biggest income losses were sustained by households in the top 1 percent of the income distribution. Those households saw a 27 percent drop in both their pre- and posttax incomes. In all other income groups the proportional drop in posttax, posttransfer income was substantially smaller than the drop in gross market income. Lower taxes and higher transfer payments erased all the market income losses suffered by households in the bottom two-fifths of the income distribution. According to CBO's estimates, households in the bottom one-fifth of the income distribution saw a small rise in their after-tax incomes even though they suffered an 8 percent drop in their average market incomes. (The CBO estimates show, however, that households in the bottom income group derive a large share of their total income from public transfers.) Middle- and lower-middle-income households saw large declines in their pretax market incomes, but when tax reductions and increased government transfers are taken into account, the percentage loss in net income was far smaller. Only near the top of the income distribution did households experience proportional losses in their after-tax incomes that were comparable to the reductions in their market incomes. The CBO income analysis thus confirms a little-known fact: The nation's social safety net as well as the special fiscal measures enacted early in the Great Recession offset a sizable fraction of the market income losses suffered by Americans in the bottom 95 percent of the income distribution. Even though many voters appear to have missed this beneficent effect of the stimulus program, the reduction in spendable income losses represents a signal achievement of U.S. fiscal policy in the Great Recession.

HOW DID FISCAL POLICY FAIL?

If fiscal policy succeeded in offsetting much of the market income loss suffered by lower- and middle-income Americans, it nonetheless failed to create buoyant demand for goods and services produced in the United States. This failure is almost certainly connected to the fact that, even in the winter of 2009, few policymakers or public or private forecasters anticipated the severity of the Great Recession. The United States had experienced severe recessions in the earlier postwar period—notably in 1974–1976 and 1980–1983—and it had seen weak recoveries after both the 1990 and 2001 recessions. But never before in the postwar period did the nation experience a severe recession followed by a painfully slow recovery. The Great Recession combined these two elements. Even in winter 2009, forecasters in the private sector, the CBO, the Federal Reserve, and the new Obama administration substantially underestimated the severity of the recession.[5] Their prediction errors were understandable—after all, they were based on the experience of other recessions in the postwar era.

The forecasting errors had unfortunate consequences. Because the reality turned out to be considerably worse than the forecast, naïve or unscrupulous critics tended to blame the disappointing outcome on the policies adopted by Congress and the Obama administration. As critics correctly pointed out, the actual trend in both output and employment turned out worse than the administration forecast. But rather than draw the correct inference—the downturn was worse than forecasters believed based on preliminary and incomplete statistics—critics of U.S. policy reached the profoundly wrong conclusion that countercyclical fiscal and monetary policy produced the disappointing shortfall.

Prudent policymakers, even if they accepted the consensus forecast, should have formulated a Plan B. They should have asked, "Suppose the outcome is much worse than we expect? Suppose unemployment rises more than forecast and payrolls rebound more slowly?" Under those circumstances, we should have expected long-term unemployment to increase substantially. Past experience shows that employers are reluctant to hire the long-term unemployed as long as there are plenty of short-term unemployed and new job seekers in the applicant queue. What policies would help deal with the swelling number of long-term unemployed? I do not think influential policymakers ever devised a Plan B. Once it was clear in summer 2009 that the financial system was on the road to recovery, the sense of crisis passed.

Some economists in the administration and many more who were advising Republican presidential aspirants and members of Congress turned to the task of trimming the deficit. They thought the crisis was over. For the growing number of long-term unemployed and the millions who would eventually join their ranks, a weak job market was or would become the central problem of their economic lives.

The simple explanation for stubbornly high unemployment was that there was too little aggregate demand for goods and services produced in the United States. The drop in overall demand due to shrunken household wealth, the sharp fall-off in the demand for new homes, and weaker business demand for new investment caused labor demand to fall far below the level needed to produce full employment. Using conventional monetary policy tools, there was little the Fed could do to boost demand once interest rates on safe short-term securities fell almost to zero. The usual policy remedy when the nation has exhausted standard monetary policy tools is to use fiscal policy to lift overall demand. The U.S. government boosted fiscal stimulus in 2008–2010 and then began to reduce that stimulus though the unemployment rate remained above 8 percent through August 2012.

Ingredients of Plan B

A more sensible policy would have aimed at boosting the demand for jobless workers well past the date when Congress began cutting the fiscal stimulus. Since voters and lawmakers were concerned about additions to the national debt, fiscal policy should have focused on reducing the country's underemployment problem. This means that every $100 added to the national debt to finance the plan should have increased by at least $100 the amount employers spent on wages and fringe benefits of workers residing in this country. Boosting transfer payments to persons and cutting business and consumer taxes are not the most reliable ways to maximize the impact of additional public spending on labor compensation.

Consumers whose disposable incomes are increased by a tax cut may spend their extra incomes on goods produced in another country, they may reduce their indebtedness, or they may increase their bank balances. If financial institutions are unwilling to lend out the extra deposits for current consumption or investment, the additional $100 in federal debt accumulated to provide the tax cut will not yield an additional $100 of outlays on wages.

The same is true of tax cuts or benefit hikes that consumers use to buy products produced in China, Thailand, or Germany. When we implement an emergency Plan B, it is with the understanding that we are trying to extricate the U.S. economy from a serious domestic crisis. We want the additions to debt to deal first and foremost with our domestic economic problem rather than the ones faced by the Chinese, Thai, or German governments. After 2009, voters and members of Congress became worried about the soaring national debt (wrongly, in my view). If we want to economize on the additions to the national debt while at the same time dealing with the shortfall in U.S. aggregate demand, we should adopt emergency policies that maximize the employment effect of each additional dollar of debt needed to deal with the shortfall. Added debt-financed spending should reduce the number of involuntarily unemployed Americans as much as possible. When there is persistent excess unemployment and widespread fear of taking on added debt, we want any additions to our debt to produce added labor income for workers in the United States rather than in other countries.

What policies could have achieved this goal? Investing in additional new or refurbished public infrastructure seems like a promising way to boost demand for U.S. workers. Both construction and durable manufacturing were badly hurt by the downturn. Payroll employment during the recession fell more than 20 percent in durable goods manufacturing and nearly 30 percent in the construction industry. Both industries were in fact already shrinking when the Great Recession began. Skilled and unskilled workers in these industries could have been put to work on useful public projects without depriving the private sector of workers whose talents were in short supply. Private sector demand for these workers was inadequate in 2009–2013 and remained inadequate through 2014.

A federal policy of funding public infrastructure could only be effective in reducing joblessness if employers added net new jobs that otherwise would not have been created. A sizable share of public infrastructure is financed, built, or maintained by state and local governments. If the federal government provides $100 billion to state governments for new infrastructure investment, it should place restrictions on the grants so states do not subtract $100 billion from infrastructure investment they otherwise would have paid for themselves. Ensuring that grantees do not offset the intended effects of grants by undertaking less self-financed activity of the kind subsidized by the grants is a well-known problem in public finance. How can the national government create incentives for state and local lawmakers to undertake new activities on their own with their own resources? Some methods have proven more effective than others. The federal government can place a floor on states' and localities' own spending on the activity it is trying to encourage. That floor can be linked to the prerecession level of state and local spending on the activity. States can then be penalized with reduced federal grant payments if state and local government outlays on the activity drops beneath the specified floor. This method of incentivizing state lawmakers is particularly effective if the increase in federal aid is expected to be temporary. Congress can also establish drop-dead dates for the expenditure of emergency federal aid. For example, Congress could have required that federal aid appropriated and authorized in 2009 must be spent no later than December 2013. Unexpended funds would then be returned to the Treasury, which could redistribute the funds to states that spent their stimulus grants on the designated activity and on schedule.

Most voters may have been under the impression that, aside from bank bailouts, the bulk of stimulus spending was devoted to infrastructure investment and maintenance projects. That is not the case. Consider the programs authorized by Congress in February 2009 as part of the American Recovery and Reinvestment Act (ARRA). Figure 3.11 presents a three-way breakdown of the fund allocations. The bottom portion of each bar shows the funds authorized for public infrastructure projects or grants and tax incentives for businesses and nonprofit organizations to invest in buildings and research and development. The appropriated funds are divided into two time periods, fiscal years 2009–2010 and 2011–2019. An overwhelming share of the total funds were expected to be spent in 2009–2010, that is, before October 2010. This is not the case, however, for the funds slated for infrastructure and R&D investments. Most of those capital expenditures were expected to be spent after 2010. These capital expenditures may be what many voters have in mind when they refer to "stimulus spending." In fact, such spending was a minor part of the stimulus. The overwhelming share of stimulus funds were spent on temporary tax cuts and transfers to persons. The share devoted to those items is indicated in the middle portion of the bars. Actually, the chart understates the fraction of stimulus dollars devoted to tax cuts and transfer benefit increases because it excludes the sizable tax cuts and benefit improvements authorized in the last year

**Figure 3.11 Anticipated Stimulus Spending under the American
Recovery and Reinvestment Act of 2009, 2009–2019**

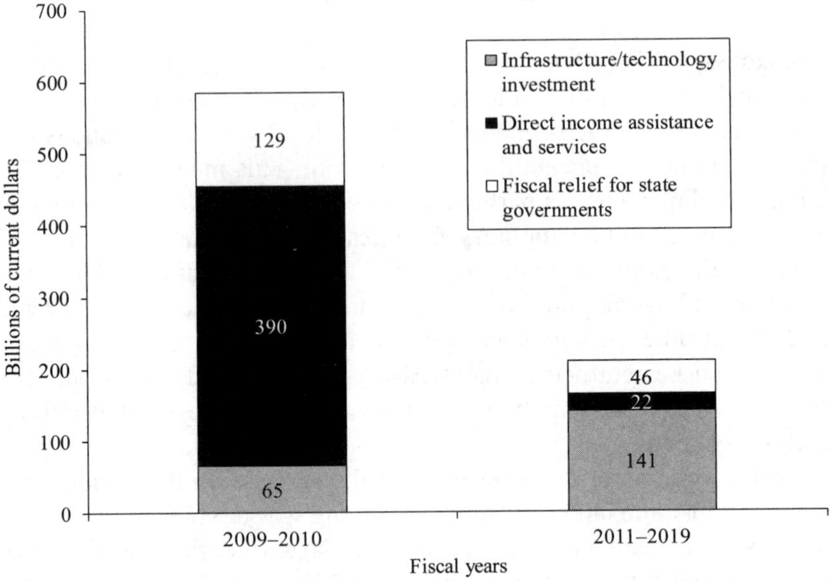

SOURCE: Author's tabulations of data from Congressional Budget Office (2009).

of the Bush administration and in the months after February 2009. It ignores all stimulus funds except those that were authorized under the ARRA program. Virtually all of the non-ARRA stimulus spending took the form of tax cuts and unemployment benefit expansions.

Why was so little money devoted to public capital projects, even though these have powerful advantages in ensuring that funds are used to buy goods and services produced in the United States? When the stimulus program was authorized, the Obama administration and well-informed members of Congress recognized they wanted the money to be spent quickly, when the slump was actually in progress. Informed policymakers were also aware of the difficulties of spending funds quickly when the money is allocated to new or refurbished public capital projects. It is hard to come up with a controversy-free list of projects on which to spend extra federal dollars. Even after a list of projects is chosen, it may take many months or even years before the resources can be invested to complete the projects. States and local governments may game the federal rules so they obtain fiscal relief with federal aid rather than add to the number of worthwhile projects they undertake or complete.

Delays in selecting and beginning capital projects will delay the expenditure of capital project funds. Federal stimulus dollars may not actually get spent until the economic emergency is past, at which point the federal dollars will compete with private-sector dollars to obtain the resources needed to complete the long-delayed projects. Skilled workers, expensive machinery, and experienced managers may be in short supply when the federal aid dollars are finally spent. Instead of boosting aggregate demand when the economy is far below full employment, the funds may get spent when the economy is near full employment. In short, funds will be spent too late to speed the recovery and just in time to fuel inflation in a fully employed economy. In contrast, tax cuts and transfer increases can be temporary and targeted on population groups in greatest need of aid.

These are valid lessons from the nation's post–World War II experience with countercyclical public works programs. They represent costly and hard-won lessons, but they do not apply with much force when policymakers are looking for a Plan B, a strategy that will reduce excess unemployment when short-term interest rates are at or near zero. In those circumstances, monetary policy will be less effective in bringing the economy closer to full employment. When the shortfall from full employment is expected to last a long time, the advantages of a temporary public works program seem compelling. Even if state and local governments cannot immediately find or begin new shovel-ready projects, they should be capable of finding and beginning them within a couple of years. The limitations mentioned above might mean few dollars would have been spent on public capital projects in 2008 or 2009. As it turned out, however, the U.S. job market still needed a sizable boost in 2010—and in 2011, 2012, 2013, and 2014. The majority of states and thousands of local governments could have found worthwhile capital projects on which to spend emergency federal aid dollars over such a lengthy span of years. The risk that such a capital investment program would have generated excess inflation now seems far-fetched, but even if we assume that states only began spending their emergency public works money when the recovery was nearly complete, policymakers can use many policy tools to reduce excess inflation. For example, the Fed could raise short-term interest rates, or Congress could raise tax rates or curb public spending on other discretionary budget items.

The third main budget category in the 2009 ARRA package was an allocation to aid state and local governments. Those funds are indicated by the top portion of the columns in Figure 3.11. The amount of money allocated to state aid in 2009–2010 was twice the level allocated to government capital projects and in research and development investment. Federal policymakers were worried in 2009 that a sharp decline in state and local revenues would push local lawmakers to cut benefits to the unemployed, trim health and education spending, and shrink public payrolls. The temporary fiscal relief from the federal government was large enough to offset a quarter to a third of the expected state and local budget imbalances that resulted from the recession. It is an open question whether this aid to state and local governments was effective in reducing employment losses in the downturn or in speeding growth in the recovery. Years of careful research will be needed to determine how states and localities spent the extra federal funds they received. State and local public employee payrolls increased modestly through the middle of 2010, and it seems likely these payroll gains would have been smaller in the absence of the temporary federal aid. State and local payrolls began to fall in 2010 at the same time private-sector employment began to recover. Public payrolls then continued to slide through the end of 2013, offsetting about one-seventh of the employment gains generated by private employers.

Figure 3.12 divides the ARRA stimulus package into the same three categories described in Figure 3.11 and shows the timing of spending on each item measured as a percentage of potential GDP in the indicated fiscal year. Total spending on the package was estimated to be $835 billion spread over 10 years. Outlays were expected to peak in fiscal year 2010 and then slide steeply immediately thereafter. However, Congress later authorized further extensions in unemployment benefits and sizable (though shrinking) tax cuts after the expiration of those authorized in ARRA. Nearly all the later stimulus packages either cut Americans' taxes (income taxes and Social Security payroll taxes) or provided more generous unemployment benefits than are offered under regular state programs. Congress failed to authorize any more capital projects or additional fiscal relief for state and local governments. A

Figure 3.12 Anticipated Stimulus Spending under the American Recovery and Reinvestment Act of 2009, 2009–2015

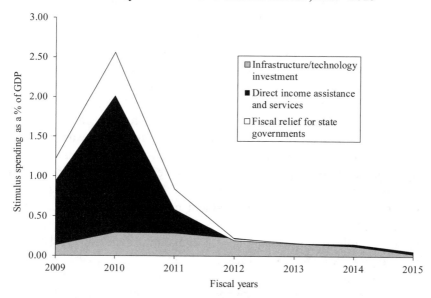

SOURCE: Author's tabulations of data from Congressional Budget Office (2009).

visual adjustment in Figure 3.12 to reflect all the stimulus programs through 2014 rather than just the spending authorized under ARRA would show much higher funding in FYs 2011–2013 for direct income assistance, provided largely in the form of tax cuts and unemployment benefit increases.

The composition of spending authorized under the stimulus packages makes public hostility to the spending puzzling. In January 2010, CNN conducted a poll asking Americans about their views of the stimulus program passed less than a year earlier (CNN 2010). The poll results showed that about 75 percent of Americans thought at least half of the stimulus dollars were "wasted" and 45 percent thought "most" or "nearly all" of the stimulus dollars had been wasted. When one considers how the stimulus outlays were allocated, this view seems extremely odd. Most of the stimulus dollars were spent directly on them, that is, the poll respondents themselves. By far the biggest slice of stimulus outlays was devoted to personal income tax cuts (lower tax withholdings or bigger refund checks). Lower direct taxes boosted after-tax incomes for at least 80 percent of American households. Other portions of the package funded extensions in unemployment benefits, hikes in food stamps, and a variety of tax credits for low-income wage earners or families rearing children. If these stimulus dollars were wasted, most of the waste was being done by the poll respondents themselves.

Another slice of stimulus spending, at least in 2009 and 2010, went to grants in aid for state spending on education and Medicaid. It is likely that only part of this aid was used by states to increase or maintain their spending on education and health benefits. A large portion was probably used for general budgetary support and indirectly to help states avoid imposing tax hikes. If polling respondents were correct and "more than half" or "nearly all" of these stimulus dollars were wasted, the blame lies not with Congress or the president but with state and local lawmakers and governors, who were provided with an additional $130 billion in federal aid with which they could maintain state and local spending or delay tax increases on local residents.

Since voters rarely object to tax reductions or transfer increases that directly benefit themselves, I suspect many poll respondents believed—erroneously—that most stimulus spending was used to pay for unpopular bank and automaker bailouts, wasteful public works projects, or generously subsidized loans to politically connected businesses. The fact that very little stimulus money was spent in this way was probably known to only a small minority of voters.

GOVERNMENT CONSUMPTION AND INVESTMENT

Many Americans may be under the impression that the federal government is still spending large amounts of money on what is popularly referred to as stimulus. Aside from very modest extra spending on transfer payments, this is not the case. Spending on public investment—roads, bridges, school and college buildings, ports, medical labs, and sewer systems—is done at the state and local level. The federal government is primarily responsible for investment in defense. Figure 3.13 shows the trend in real spending on state and local government investment in the two worst recessions of the postwar era. The solid

Figure 3.13 State and Local Government Investment in Two Postwar Recessions

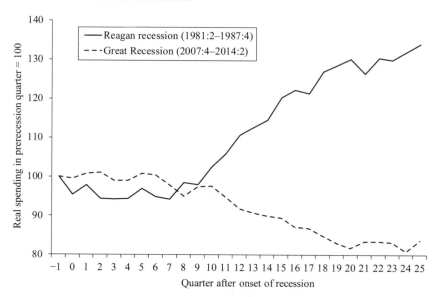

SOURCE: Dept. of Commerce, Bureau of Economic Analysis, National Income and Product Accounts.

line shows the trend in real state and local spending on public investment during and after the recession of the early 1980s, and the dashed line shows the same trend during and after the Great Recession. In the recent recession, state spending on public investment projects held up well when federal stimulus dollars were directly supporting state budgets, but state and local investment began to shrink starting in the seventh quarter after the onset of the recession. State and local investment spending has recently been one-fifth below its prerecession level. In contrast, it shrank about 5 percent during the recession in the early 1980s but then began to recover. Six years after the start of the recession, state and local investment spending was one-third higher than it was prior.

Statistics on total government outlays on final consumption and investment are equally depressing. Figure 3.14 shows the trend in this form of public spending at all levels of government—federal, state,

Figure 3.14 Total Government Final Consumption and Gross Investment in Two Postwar Recessions

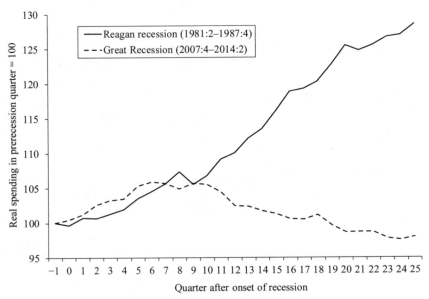

SOURCE: Dept. of Commerce, Bureau of Economic Analysis, National Income and Product Accounts.

and local. This spending includes not only national defense and non-defense investment, but also the compensation payments to government employees and contractors. The solid line in the chart shows the trend in spending in the recession of the 1980s. Even though the national government in that era was politically conservative, real spending rose steadily and substantially during and after the economic downturn. In the Great Recession, the stimulus packages initially pushed up government consumption and investment outlays, but by the tenth quarter after the onset of the recession, spending already began to decline. By the nineteenth quarter after the recession began, government consumption and investment was 2 percent below its prerecession level. At the same point in the recovery from the 1980s recession, real spending was 27 percent higher than it was before the recession began. During the Great Recession, shrinking government budgets during the recovery tended to depress overall demand; during the 1980s recession, steady increases in government spending throughout the recovery boosted aggregate demand. Even though unemployment remained high and utilization of the capital stock low, policymakers began to shrink public consumption and investment soon after 2009. By 2013 real government spending on these items was smaller than it was when the recession began.

Starting in 2010 advocates of government austerity may have believed it was prudent to refrain from borrowing additional funds because savers inside and outside the United States were growing frightened of the nation's mounting public debt. Some stimulus critics feared that current and future U.S. taxpayers would have to pay extraordinarily high interest rates to borrow the funds needed to finance public budgets. This fear seems nonsensical in view of the interest rates actually paid on U.S. government debt. One indicator of the burden future taxpayers will have to pay is the real interest rate savers demand in order to hold U.S. Treasury securities. The world's savers do not demand that the United States pay much interest on its public debt. Figure 3.15 shows the trend in real interest rates on five-year and long-duration indexed U.S. Treasury securities. For most of the 2011–2014 period, the five-year indexed bond offered a yield of less than 0 percent. Savers offered to lend the federal government funds for five years and receive interest payments that did not even compensate them for the change in the price level. The chart also displays the trend in real yields on long-duration inflation-indexed Treasury securities.[6] In the first four years after the financial crisis the yield on these long-duration securities fell from 2.5 percent to 0.0 percent. In the last quarter of 2012 savers in effect offered to hold federal debt without receiving any real compensation at all. Based on the evidence in Figure 3.15, it is hard to see any evidence that savers were losing confidence in the government's ability to repay its debt.

If the government can find investment projects that are expected to yield benefits that exceed 1 or 2 percent a year over the next 15–20 years, it would be worthwhile to invest in those projects. Savers were offering (and continue to offer) the federal government funds at historically low interest rates at the same time the nation had millions of unemployed workers and a sizable amount of unused productive capacity.

It is hard to believe the country cannot identify infrastructure projects with payoffs that are expected to yield 1 or 2 percent a year. According to the World Economic Forum's most recent *Global Competitiveness Report* (Schwab 2013), infrastructure in the United States

Figure 3.15 Real Yields on U.S. Treasury Inflation-Indexed Securities, 2003–2014

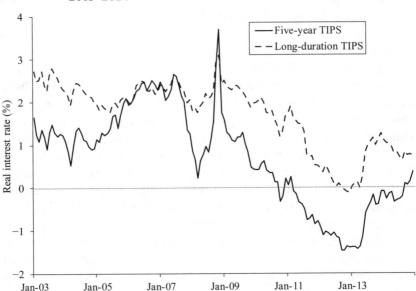

SOURCE: Board of Governors of the U.S. Federal Reserve System.

ranks fifteenth among the countries graded. This is a somewhat higher rank than Austria and a lower rank than Korea and Taiwan. Each of the other countries has substantially lower average incomes than the United States, so one might expect the United States to have substantially better infrastructure.

The fact that it does not suggests there are many attractive opportunities to improve or add to U.S. infrastructure. It is easy to identify types of infrastructure that need improvement or repair. Every four years the American Society of Civil Engineers offers a detailed assessment of U.S. infrastructure, detailing its strengths and shortcomings across a number of categories, including dams, drinking water systems, wastewater, bridges, inland waterways, and ports (see, for example, American Society of Civil Engineers [2013]). The report pinpoints areas where current spending on maintenance falls short of the level needed to keep the infrastructure operating at a constant level. For many kinds of infrastructure, of course, a growing population and heavier demands require that we invest in new facilities. There was no better time for such investment than the years immediately following the financial crisis. The government's borrowing cost for investment spending was near a historical low, and the labor and capital resources needed to produce additional investment were not being used by households and private businesses. The failure to use fiscal policy, particularly public investment policy, to bring the nation closer to full employment after 2009, represents the most notable failure of policymaking in the Great Recession. It produced unnecessary suffering for the nation's long-term unemployed, and it wasted a rare opportunity to improve or rebuild the nation's public infrastructure at very low cost.

EXPLANATIONS

Policymakers failed to use fiscal policy adequately to deal with the slump that followed the 2008 financial crisis. At least two factors contributed to this failure. First, technical forecasts of the economic fallout from the crisis understated its ultimate severity. Many analysts may have believed that when confidence in financial institutions and financial markets was restored, the nonfinancial economy would rebound quickly as normal credit flows resumed. For tens of millions of households, however, a functioning financial system did not restore their access to credit. For many, their primary asset was their home, and that home was worth much less after 2007 than it was before. Fixing the financial system did not repair the balance sheets of households that borrowed heavily to purchase homes that lost a large share of their value.

By the time forecasters and decision-makers recognized that consumer and business demand would not rebound quickly, the political window for enacting an appropriately scaled fiscal program had closed. Many voters accepted the verdict that the stimulus program had failed. More to the point, they elected politicians to the House of Representatives committed to the idea that additional stimulus would put the creditworthiness of the United States at risk. Many politicians who were most committed to addressing the nation's unemployment problem through fiscal policy lost in the 2010, 2012, and 2014 elections.

Of course, the belief that a stimulus program is needed depends crucially on the weight one assigns to the well-being of jobless workers and the underemployed. If the distress of the unemployed ranks at the top of voters' concerns, policymakers may be willing to adopt strong antirecession measures, even if the policies carry some risk or have unpopular side effects such as a larger public debt. In many western democracies voters care most intensely about the unemployed when long-term unemployment is a plausible risk they face themselves. At that point, job loss is not a risk facing some anonymous stranger. It is a risk that represents a real possibility for themselves or a family member, neighbor, or friend. The Great Recession was like other postwar recessions, both in the United States and in other rich democracies. Workers' fear of losing their job spiked with the layoff rate and the number of front-page stories about new mass layoffs. These stories fall off the front page and out of the news cycle when the layoff rate declines, as it inevitably does. The suffering of the unemployed slips from voters' consciousness and seems less urgent to policymakers.

We saw this in Western Europe in the late 1980s, and I suspect our great-grandparents also saw it in the late 1930s. In late-1980s Europe and late-1930s America, the unemployment rate remained stubbornly high, but layoffs were no longer an immediate concern of workers who managed to hang on to their jobs or find new ones. The simple fact is that a high level of long-term unemployment is not mainly the result of a high current layoff rate but rather the result of the failure of private and public employers to create enough new jobs to reemploy long-time job seekers and to provide plentiful work opportunities for school leavers. Even when the unemployment rate holds steady at 15 percent, it takes a great deal of empathy on the part of voters who are safely employed to place a high weight on the welfare of strangers who have been without work for a long time. Workers' altruism toward the unemployed gets a lift when the layoff rate soars, but when this moment passes, as it did after 2009, the welfare of the unemployed sinks lower among the concerns of both voters and elected officials. After the moment passes, it may be hard to persuade voters that further sacrifices for the unemployed are needed.

Although voters' fears about the economic consequences of a larger public debt were baseless, they may have been decisive in shifting the priorities of policymakers toward fiscal austerity and away from further stimulus. That shift slowed the recovery and worsened the prospects of the long-term unemployed as well as young adults trying to begin their careers. While those two groups experienced unnecessary additional pain as a result of the pivot toward austerity, it is hard to see how the policy shift had a beneficial payoff for the voters whose election day choices produced the policy shift.

Notes

1. http://www.nber.org/cycles.html (accessed October 29, 2014).
2. Atif, Rao, and Sufi (2013) offer a somewhat larger estimate of the expected loss in consumption based on their finding that households with lower net worth and higher leverage ratios cut spending more aggressively in response to a decline in wealth.
3. http://www.federalreserve.gov/econresdata/scf/files/scf2013_tables_internal _real.xls (accessed December 1, 2014).
4. Workers earning less than the average wage obtain compensation for a larger fraction of their earnings loss, while those earning higher wages receive proportionately less generous compensation (Burtless and Gordon 2011; Immervoll and Richardson 2013).
5. In February 2009 the White House published a comparison of the 2009 and 2010 projections of a number of forecasters. The administration predicted a year-over-year change in GDP of −1.2 percent; the CBO's prediction was −0.9 percent; and the consensus Blue Chip forecast was −1.6 percent. The actual change in real GDP was −2.8 percent (the White House 2009).
6. This represents the average bid yields for all Treasury inflation-protected securities with remaining terms to maturity of 10 years or more.

References

American Society of Civil Engineers. 2013. *2013 Report Card for America's Infrastructure*. Reston, VA: ASCE. http://infrastructurereportcard.org (accessed August 30, 2016).

Atif, Mian, Kamalesh Rao, and Amir Sufi. 2013. "Household Balance Sheets, Consumption, and the Economic Slump." *Quarterly Journal of Economics* 128(4): 1687–1726.

Board of Governors of the Federal Reserve System. n.d. Survey of Consumer Finances. Table 4: Family Net Worth by Selected Characteristics of Families, 1989–2013 Surveys. Washington, DC: Board of Governors of the Fed-

eral Reserve System. http://www.federalreserve.gov/econresdata/scf/files/
scf2013_tables_internal_real.xls (accessed August 30, 2016).

Burtless, Gary, and Tracy Gordon. 2011. "The Federeal Stimulus Programs
and Their Effects." In *The Great Recession*, David B. Grusky, Bruce
Western, and Christopher Wimer, eds. New York: Russell Sage Foundation,
pp. 249–293.

CNN. 2010. "CNN Poll: Three of Four Americans Say Much of Stimulus
Money Wasted." January 25. http://www.cnn.com/2010/POLITICS/01/25/
poll.stimulus.money/ and http://i2.cdn.turner.com/cnn/2010/images/01/25/
rel1g.pdf (accessed August 30, 2016).

Congressional Budget Office (CBO). 2009. "Letter to the Honorable Nancy
Pelosi," Tables 1 and 2. February 13. Washington, DC: CBO. https://www
.cbo.gov/sites/default/files/111th-congress-2009-2010/costestimate/
hr1conference0.pdf (accessed September 21, 2017).

———. 2014. "The Distribution of Household Income and Federal Taxes,
2011." Washington, DC: CBO. http://www.cbo.gov/publication/49440
(accessed August 30, 2016).

Immervoll, Herwig, and Linda Richardson. 2013. "Redistribution Policy in
Europe and the United States: Is the Great Recession a 'Game Changer' for
Working-age Families?" OECD Social, Employment, and Migration Work-
ing Paper No. 150. Paris: OECD.

National Bureau of Economic Research. N.d. "U.S. Business Cycle Expansions
and Contractions." Cambridge, MA: NBER. http://www.nber.org/cycles
.html (accessed August 30, 2016).

Schwab, Klaus. 2013. *The Global Competitiveness Report, 2013–2014*.
Geneva: World Economic Forum. http://www3.weforum.org/docs/WEF
_GlobalCompetitivenessReport_2013-2014.pdf (check link).

White House. 2009. "Economic Projections and the Budget Outlook." Washington, DC: White House. http://www.whitehouse.gov/assets/documents/
Economic_Projections_and_the_Budget_Outlook.pdf (accessed August
30, 2016).

4

Central Banking
in the Great Recession

New Policies, Old Principles

Donald Kohn
Brookings Institution

In 2007 and 2008 the U.S. financial markets and economy were hit with a series of huge shocks. As shown in Figure 4.1, house prices started to fall in the summer of 2006 and eventually declined by an average of 35 percent. A superstructure of mortgage lending that had been built on the expectation of ever-rising house prices began to unravel. Mortgage loans had been made to increasingly unqualified borrowers and for speculative purposes, and it gradually became evident to lenders—and more importantly, creditors of lenders—that these loans would not be repaid and that the underlying collateral in many cases would be worth less than what was owed on the loans, leaving lenders to incur losses. Complicating the picture greatly was the fact that these loans had been bundled into securities and then sliced and diced and resold so that no one could be sure where the losses would fall. In the resulting financial panic and recession, equity prices fell by almost half, and the unemployment rate rose from 4.75 percent to over 10 percent (see Figures 4.2 and 4.3).

Ben Bernanke, former chairman of the Federal Reserve, and other observers have noted that the initial shock, including the doubts about the viability of financial institutions, was larger than that which started the Great Depression. Many economists, including Bernanke, have attributed the extent and duration of the Great Depression importantly to the failure of the Federal Reserve to counter the emerging problems aggressively enough. This chapter focuses on what the Federal Reserve did in the Great Recession of 2007–2009 to avoid a repeat. To this end, it undertook a series of unconventional and largely unprecedented

Figure 4.1 House Prices, 2007–2011

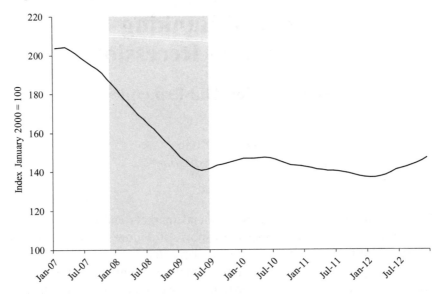

SOURCE: S&P Dow Jones Indices LLC.

Figure 4.2 Equity Prices, 2007–2009

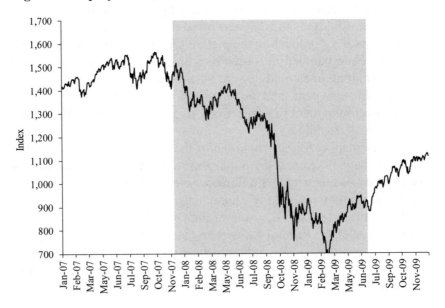

SOURCE: S&P Dow Jones Indices LLC.

Figure 4.3 Unemployment Rate, 2007–2011

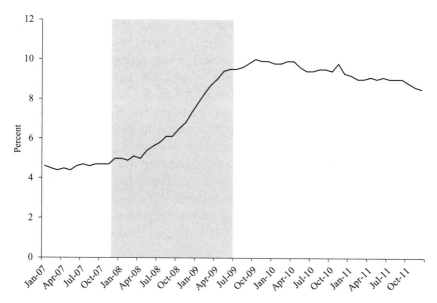

SOURCE: U.S. Department of Labor, Bureau of Labor Statistics.

policy actions. But my hypothesis is that these actions did not come from nowhere; rather, they were natural extensions of policies utilized in more normal times, founded on past central bank behavior and lessons learned from previous experience in tough times, here and in other countries. I was the vice chairman of the Federal Reserve Board from 2006 to 2010, and this account is based in part on my first-hand experience contributing to the formulation and implementation of many of these unconventional policies.

POLICYMAKING IN A CRISIS

From several perspectives, managing a crisis is extraordinarily challenging. Although the Fed could and did take some broad lessons from history, the few precedents for the situation in the United States were either very old or occurred in financial systems that were much different (the Depression) or much milder (the financial shocks of the 1980s and 1990s). In addition, the policymakers did not know the true state of the world. Market participants and the Federal Reserve were working with stale information about lenders and borrowers from outdated balance sheets and income statements. The supervisors at the Fed could supply more up to date analysis and information, but the situation was evolving rapidly, important institutions under fire were not banks and hadn't been subject to close oversight, and people in the private sector supplying new information often had vested interests in pushing the Fed toward one policy choice or another. We could observe what was going on in markets, but market prices were driven by fear and panic and did not represent underlying values that were likely to prevail over time. The lack of precedent and knowledge of the true state of the world meant that the Fed was operating largely under Knightian uncertainty— a circumstance in which it could not make good estimates of the probabilities of particular outcomes.

We had one critical advantage: Ben Bernanke's leadership. One aspect of that good fortune was his leadership style. He remained calm under severe stress, providing an anchor for the rest of us. And he was open to new ideas—sending out "blue sky" emails with lots of suggestions on new approaches and soliciting the views of others.

In addition, Bernanke is a leading scholar of the Great Depression, and he was well aware of the ways that financial crises propagate through the economic system. He was also aware of the mistakes the Federal Reserve had made that allowed that propagation to occur in the 1930s, resulting in an economic crisis of unprecedented length and severity. In a 90th birthday celebration for Milton Friedman well before the most recent crisis, Bernanke noted that, thanks to Friedman and his coauthor, economist Anna Schwartz, we now understood what we—the Fed—had done wrong in the Depression, we were very sorry, and we promised we wouldn't let it happen again. The story of 2007–2009 is what the Fed under Bernanke's leadership did to make good on that promise.

The Federal Reserve devised many unconventional and innovative policies to counter the effects of the crisis, but they were based on extensions of tried and true central bank policy tools. Those tools fell into two broad categories—lending by the Fed through its discount window and lowering interest rates in the conduct of monetary policy.

The two policies are not entirely separable: for example, lending at the discount window increased the Fed's balance sheet and led to lower interest rates, and the more successful one type of policy was the less pressure on the other. But they did have different origins, and this chapter covers each type separately.

LENDING

Large segments of the financial sector are inherently fragile, reflecting what we expect from it. When we give it our savings we often want to be able to get them back quickly and with the principle intact—we want high liquidity. However, when we borrow we do so at longer terms, say, for 3–4 years to finance the purchase of a car and 30 years to buy a house, or, for a business, for several months to finance inventory or several years to finance capital equipment and buildings. So, banks and many other financial intermediaries operate with marked maturity mismatches: their liabilities—our savings—are far shorter than their assets—our borrowing. They also tend to rely very heavily on deposits or other borrowing and very little on equity, which is a more expensive source of funds, so they are highly leveraged with small cushions of equity to absorb losses on their loans and other assets. This fragile structure rests on confidence—confidence that whenever we want to access our savings—for example, to get cash from our deposit or money fund investment—we will be able to do so and get the full amount we are expecting.

When people lose confidence in the financial sector, bad things happen. They recognize that they are more likely to be able to get their funds in full and on time if they are near the head of the line; after others have withdrawn, the institution may run out of cash or assets that can readily be turned into cash. When confidence is lost, we get runs on banks or other financial intermediaries. If enough people try to get their money back, institutions will be forced to sell often illiquid assets—and sell them at any price to meet demands for cash. That results in fire sales of assets that can drive the price of the assets well below their intrinsic value.

In 2007 and 2008 the panic originated from developments in the subprime mortgage market, but that triggered much wider duress. As house prices declined, people began to realize that many lenders faced large losses. However, the mortgages had been packaged together and those packages had been broken up and repackaged in complex and opaque ways. Consequently, no one could be sure where the losses would eventually be absorbed, and there was a more general pulling back from lending to a variety of financial institutions. The financial institutions under stress needed to sell assets, driving down the price of mortgages and other assets even further, raising more questions about the viability of lenders and provoking further withdrawals. A Wall Street/financial institution death spiral was under way.

Critically, when lenders are under pressure they pull back from making new loans. Credit for households and businesses tightens up, or in the extreme dries up entirely. When we can't borrow to buy goods and services we cut back spending, which causes businesses to lay off workers, who in turn may have to default on loans and reduce spending further, deepening the recession and financial sector stress. The Wall Street death spiral becomes a Main Street death spiral.

The central bank's tools to deal with a Main Street death spiral are limited. The Fed can't step in and lend directly to households and businesses—it is not equipped to make those types of decisions, and we wouldn't want an institution that is both public sector and politically independent closely involved in allocating credit by picking and choosing among loan applicants. What it can do is intervene in the financial sector, reducing the pressure on banks and other institutions to end the runs and fire sales and keep credit flowing to Main Street.

The person who first recognized and formulated the policy for the central bank in a panic was Walter Bagehot, and he did so in the middle of the nineteenth century, after watching the Bank of England deal with financial panics in the City of London. He said the central bank should lend to banks and other institutions freely so they can meet deposit withdrawals and pay back lenders. Central banks should lend against illiquid but still good collateral, giving the banks a source of funds they could access without engaging in fires sales of assets. By being ready to make liquidity available to banks and other institutions, central banks would assure depositors and other lenders that they could get their funds back when they asked for them, so they didn't need to line up to withdraw, forestalling or at least limiting panics. In effect, the central bank would provide liquidity insurance to banks and sometimes other intermediaries; special government intervention was justified by the key role financial institutions play in the broader economy, intermediating between savers and spenders and operating the payments system. Indeed, the Fed was founded in 1913 in large part because the absence of a lender of last resort had made financial panics in the late nineteenth and early twentieth centuries more destructive than they would have been if a lender had been ready to step in.

But lending freely against good collateral was not the end of Bagehot's advice or of the central bank playbook based on his recommendations. Any insurance carries moral hazard—it reduces the incentives for the buyers of the insurance to take steps to protect themselves. Two other elements in the central bank playbook for lending into a panic are designed to limit that moral hazard. First, lend only to solvent institutions; do not keep alive institutions that have made so many fundamentally bad decisions they have run through their shareholder capital. And second, charge a penalty rate relative to the rates that will prevail once market functioning is restored; higher rates mean that the central bank will be the lender of last resort—after private sector funds dry up—and will induce borrowers from the central bank to repay when markets normalize.

The Federal Reserve implemented the Bagehot-based rule book. As Figure 4.4 shows, it lent in great size during the crisis—especially after generalized market panic that followed the failure of Lehman Brothers. Total discount window lending, which is normally close to zero, shot up to nearly $1.8 trillion in early 2009. But it also lent at a penalty to market rates, so as markets stabilized and financial institutions were recapitalized by the government and in the markets, lending subsided fairly rapidly over 2009.

Although lending mostly followed the Bagehot principles, the Fed found it had to innovate in several ways to achieve its objectives of stemming the panic and promoting greater availability of credit to households and businesses. Banks are the usual counterparties of the Federal Reserve at the discount window, but banks became reluctant to use the window because they feared looking weak, which might feed a run instead of stopping it. This stigma got in the way of the Fed's ability to supply liquidity and avert credit tightening when uncertainty about

Figure 4.4 Lending by the Federal Reserve

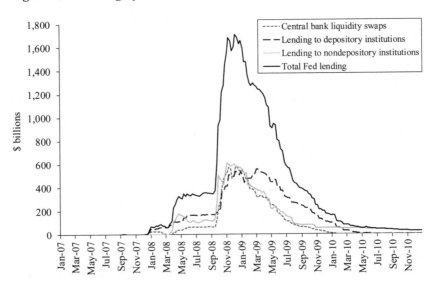

SOURCE: Federal Reserve Board, Flow of Funds.

counterparty risk disrupted interbank funding markets. It then began to make the credit to banks available in auctions in which many participated so no one stood out.

A critical characteristic of the events of 2008 was that the panic wasn't limited to the banking system. Figure 4.5 shows intermediation involving securitization of loans and money market lending outside banks themselves—dubbed the shadow banking system—rose substantially before the crisis. The securitization of mortgages meant that they were spread throughout the financial system and often not held in banks. In many respects, that was fine because risk was widely dispersed, often among long-term holders. But a lot of the pieces of securitized mortgages were held in financial structures that looked and behaved like banks in that the long-term mortgages were financed by short-term debt and backed by little if any equity to absorb losses. Some of those structures were attached in one way or another to banks and came back to them as confidence evaporated. But vulnerabilities extended well beyond the banking system, and runs spread to broker-dealers holding mortgage securities, money market funds lending to the

Figure 4.5 Shadow Banking Liabilities, 2000–2014

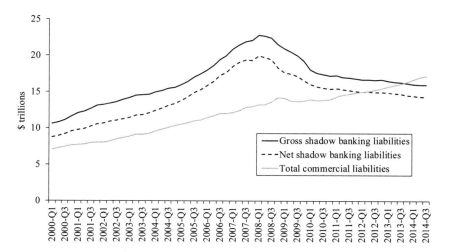

NOTE: Gross measure sums all liabilities recorded in the flow of funds that relate to securitization activity (MBS, ABS, and other GSE liabilities), as well as all short-term money market transactions that are not backstopped by deposit insurance (repos, commercial paper, and other MMMF liabilities). Net measure attempts to correct for double counting (Pozsar 2010).
SOURCE: Federal Reserve Flow of Funds, Haver Analytics.

broker-dealers, and other elements in this so-called shadow banking system. The United States is generally fortunate to have well-developed securities and securitization markets alongside its banks; they can keep the credit flowing when the banks are in trouble and not lending. But in 2008 all elements of the system were subject to runs and fire sales as confidence evaporated; the problems in the nonbanks were having serious adverse effects on the abilities of households and businesses to borrow. In response, the Federal Reserve activated an authorization to lend to nonbanks that it hadn't used since the 1930s. It lent to broker-dealers, to money market funds, to issuers of commercial paper, and to buyers of securitized debt to limit the damage to the economy from the panic afflicting financial markets.

It wasn't only problems at U.S. banks and markets that were damaging the U.S. economy; many foreign banks also were in trouble in their transactions in dollars, and that was feeding back badly on U.S.

financial markets. In the years leading up to the crisis many foreign banks, attracted by the high rates and the high ratings from the credit rating agencies, invested in pieces of subprime mortgage securitizations. These banks were funding those investments with short-term borrowings and deposits, often not in dollars but instead with domestic deposits the banks subsequently converted into dollars in short-term markets, like swap markets. As confidence in the banks waned, they lost access to swap markets, and they needed to bid more strongly directly in U.S. markets for dollars; this was putting upward pressure on U.S. interest rates at a time when the Fed was trying to hold those rates down to fight recession.

The Fed could and did lend directly to foreign banks operating in the United States at its discount window, but in many cases it didn't have the information to judge whether the borrowing bank was solvent or whether the collateral it had to offer was sound. So, the Federal Reserve lent dollars to foreign central banks to lend to their domestic banks, allowing the foreign central banks to make those difficult judgment calls. That lending between central banks was called "central bank foreign currency liquidity swaps," and the loans were unprecedented in the size and the purpose for which they were made.

I have already noted the high degree of uncertainty that faced the central bank in coping with the crisis. Of course, the private sector was dealing with the same phenomenon. In particular, lenders to financial institutions and other borrowers were concerned that they couldn't judge the depth of the likely losses in their counterparties, which could prove considerable in a period of unprecedented declines in asset prices. Lenders might be willing to take some risk, but the potential for very large losses impeded their willingness to extend funding. So, the Fed, for several of its facilities (sometimes together with the Treasury's TARP facility) took on this tail risk—it would absorb extremely large losses once the private sector had taken some losses. Although the Fed didn't take any losses of this sort, its willingness to do so helped bolster private lender confidence and restore the more normal working of the markets.

Did these lending facilities work? Yes, eventually. They didn't prevent a panic, especially after the failure of Lehman Brothers, but they did limit the extent of the damage to the markets and the economy and, by boosting confidence, helped to restore more normal functioning of the markets. They didn't prevent panic in part because the law requires that to activate lending to nonbanks, the Federal Reserve Board must find that a deeply problematic situation already prevails—the circumstances are "unusual and exigent" and credit is not otherwise available. By necessity, these nonbank facilities had to be put into place in response to panicky situations that had already developed.

Were they "bailouts"? The funds were advanced when private credit was not available, and without the Fed's lending, many more institutions would have gone under. But they were loans, not capital injections, for the most part to solvent institutions that were denied access to markets because of developments beyond their control, fully in keeping with the Bagehot principles and the intent of the writers of the Federal Reserve Act.

However, there were also borderline situations when the liquidity needs of troubled institutions were met through special facilities. These were uncomfortable for the Fed, but the authorities, including the Treasury as well as the Fed, judged that the failure of the particular institution would have had major adverse consequences for the economy, and alternative methods for dealing with the situation were not available. Now they are. The Fed strongly backed a part of Dodd-Frank that gave the FDIC, working with the Fed and other authorities, new powers to resolve troubled financial institutions without endangering the stability of the financial system. Loans to individual troubled institutions are not permitted after Dodd-Frank, but the alternative should be effective in protecting stability while allowing institutions to fail in an orderly way.

MONETARY POLICY AND INTEREST RATES

The second main strand of Federal Reserve policy in the crisis involved the setting of interest rates—monetary policy. Through its announcements and open market operations to add and subtract reserves from the banking system, the Fed exerts very close control over an overnight interest rate—the federal funds rate. As Figure 4.6 shows, in a recession, the Fed normally reduces this rate to fight unemployment and keep inflation from falling much below its target. Lowering the federal funds rate—or market expectations that it will be lowered—

Figure 4.6 Federal Funds Rate, 1973–2013

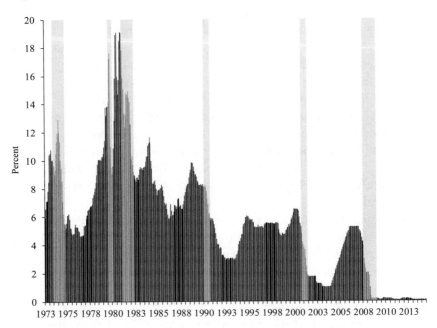

SOURCE: Federal Reserve Board and Haver Analytics.

generally leads to decreased intermediate and long-term interest rates. Lower intermediate and longer-term rates make it cheaper for people to borrow to buy cars and houses, and for businesses to finance new capital equipment and buildings. They also tend to raise asset prices, which is especially important for equities and houses because that's what constitutes household wealth, and when people are wealthier they tend to spend a little more because they don't need to save as much for the future. Lower interest rates also tend to depreciate the dollar on foreign exchange markets as investments in foreign assets look to return more relative to investments here in the United States; a lower dollar makes our exports more affordable to foreigners and makes their products less affordable for U.S. residents, shifting spending to the output of U.S. factories.

Lower interest rates, higher wealth, and a cheaper dollar all tend to boost spending. Greater spending puts people back to work, and the extra demand keeps inflation from falling below the Fed's target or causes inflation to rise once it is already below target. In the fall and winter of 2008–2009, the United States was in a deep recession, but the federal funds rate was already at zero. Fortunately, several economists, including Ben Bernanke, had thought about what to do in this situation, which Japan had been facing for some time. The advice was to intervene in the financial markets further along the chain—reduce intermediate and long-term rates directly, which in turn should stimulate spending through all the channels mentioned above—cost of credit, wealth, and exchange rates. It would also bolster confidence and encourage risk taking at a time when lenders were extremely risk averse. Two separate techniques were used to reduce intermediate- and long-term interest rates: buying longer-term debt and giving more information about policy intentions to lower expectations about the path of interest rates in the future.

The Fed called the first technique *large-scale asset purchases*, but everyone else called it *quantitative easing*. The assets purchased were mortgage-backed securities (MBS) guaranteed by Fannie Mae and Freddie Mac, securities issued by these two agencies, and U.S. Treasury bonds. The Fed started by announcing definite amounts—e.g., $1.25 trillion—but, after several iterations with specific amounts, finished with an open-ended commitment to buy long-term Treasuries and MBS at a pace of $85 billion per month until the economy had improved enough that this extraordinary action was no longer needed. In fact, purchases continued at this pace from the fall of 2012 until December 2013, after which the pace of purchases was phased down gradually (tapered) until October 2014, when they stopped altogether. As Figure 4.7 shows, the securities portfolio of the Fed had reached nearly $4.5 trillion by that time, up from under $1 trillion before the crisis.

How was this supposed to work? The purchases had several effects on markets. By increasing the demand for the long-term securities that were being purchased, they raised the price and lowered the yield. Lower yields on Treasuries and MBS caused investors to look around for other, higher-yielding, assets, such as equities and corporate bonds; and the investors who sold the Treasury bonds and MBS now had cash to redeploy to other long-term assets. In these ways, the Fed's purchases in particular segments of the securities markets were transmitted to financial markets more broadly. In addition, the announcement of the

Figure 4.7 Federal Reserve Securities Portfolio, 2002–2014

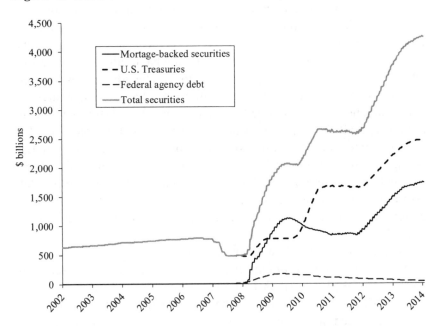

SOURCE: Federal Reserve Board.

purchases likely signaled the Federal Reserve's determination to use unconventional policies to promote a return to full employment and get inflation up to its 2 percent target, reinforcing its messages that interest rates would be low for a long time.

The second technique to lower intermediate and longer-term rates was to make that message about the expected path for the federal funds rate in the future much more explicit than usual—that is, give *forward guidance* on interest rates. The Fed used a variety of formulations of its language about the path of rates to convince markets that the rate would remain essentially at zero for quite some time—longer than market participants might otherwise have anticipated. The expected path for short-term rates is a key component in determining long-term rates, and the Fed's intention through its assurances about holding rates low for long was to lower longer-term rates—or to keep them from rising before the Fed thought it consistent with achieving its employment and inflation objectives.

Like asset purchases, the specific form of the guidance evolved over time. What began as very vague guidance—"for some time" and "for a considerable period"—shifted to more precise time-based guidance—"at least through mid-2013" and then "at least through 2014." The language became more focused on economic conditions—"at least until unemployment falls below 6.5 percent, provided inflation does not exceed the 2 percent target by more than one-half percent"—and then moved to a combination of economic conditions keyed to progress towards its objectives and time—it would be "patient" in raising rates. In 2014, it dropped the "patient" language and focused only on actual and expected progress toward its inflation and employment goals.

The Fed needed to return to these monetary policy tools multiple times over an extended period because the recovery from the very deep recession was so slow and disappointing. The Fed's legislation gives it two mandates: "maximum employment and stable prices." Maximum employment is interpreted as the highest level that can be sustained over time without promoting ever increasing inflation. That goal is usually expressed in terms of the unemployment rate—how low can it go without creating inflation problems. In 2014, the central tendency of the participants at Federal Open Market Committee meetings is that the unemployment rate could go to 5 to 5.25 percent on a sustained basis without untoward inflation developments, and that level was broadly in alignment with the estimates of many outside economists at that time. But as shown in Figure 4.8, the unemployment rate did not come down to that level until early 2015.

For stable prices the Fed has set a target of 2 percent inflation measured by the PCE deflator. That goal is plotted in Figure 4.9, along with realized inflation. The 2 percent goal is shared by many central banks around the world. It's not zero because that would risk falling into a costly deflationary spiral too often. And, inflation below 2 percent on average would mean interest rates would be very low on average, giving the Fed little room to ease its fed funds target if bad things happened to the economy.

Until 2015, the economy operated with a far weaker labor market than consistent with "maximum employment"; moreover, in the period after the crisis inflation ran consistently below the 2 percent target. The Fed anticipated that the recovery from the very deep recession would be slower than most recoveries from deep recessions. We entered the

Figure 4.8 Unemployment Relative to Full Employment, 2007–2015

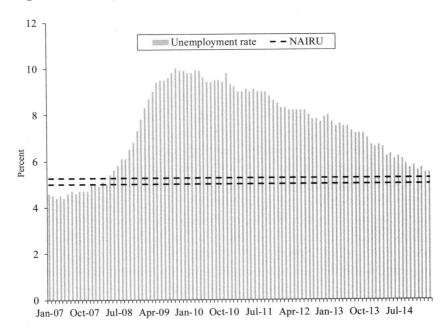

NOTE: NAIRU = Nonaccelerating inflation rate of unemployment.
SOURCE: U.S. Department of Labor, Bureau of Labor Statistics, and Federal Reserve
   Board Federal Open Market Committee minutes (for NAIRU estimates).

recession with an overhang of houses on the market, with households
having incurred unsustainable levels of debt, and with lenders having
deeply impaired balance sheets as households and businesses defaulted
on debts in the housing downturn and recession. Rebuilding balance
sheets takes time and elevated saving. But the economic expansion
has been disappointing even relative to these restrained expectations,
and inflation has persisted below target; as actual economic activity
and prices fell short, the Federal Reserve judged that it needed these
repeated rounds of policy easing to hit its legislated goals.

   Given that disappointment, *did the policy easing work?* The studies of the Fed's announcements on financial conditions generally have
shown that the actions were effective in lowering interest rates and raising asset prices. The effects might have been greatest in the Treasury

Figure 4.9 Inflation Relative to Federal Reserve Target, 2007–2015

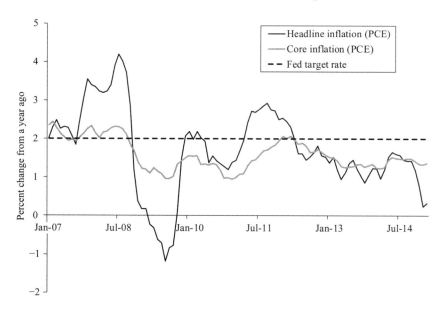

SOURCE: Bureau of Economic Analysis and Federal Reserve Board Federal Open Market Committee minutes (for target estimates).

and MBS markets, where the purchases were made, but they seem to have fed through to some extent into other markets where households and businesses borrow and invest. What is much harder to show, not surprisingly considering the lackluster recovery, is that the lower interest rates and higher equity prices had a substantially positive effect on spending. Models drawing on historical relationships say they did, and so does the logic in this chapter. Some of the "headwinds" the economy faced were not anticipated—for example, eurozone problems beginning in 2010, restrictive U.S. fiscal policy in 2012 and 2013, and very tight credit conditions continuing for longer than expected in residential real estate markets. I believe that the recovery and expansion would have been even weaker than we experienced if the Fed had not been so aggressive.

CONCLUSION

Ben Bernanke said during the crisis that he didn't agree with some of what Franklin Roosevelt did to get out of the Depression, but he admired Roosevelt's determination to try new things until something worked. That was one lesson underlined by the Fed's response to the crisis: in unprecedented circumstances, innovate until you find something effective. At the same time, those innovations need to be based on deep thinking about the nature of the problems and the tools at hand to deal with them. The Fed couldn't inject capital into the financial system—that was for TARP—but it could supply liquidity very broadly, and it could ease financial conditions through a variety of techniques to lower interest rates in order to stimulate spending.

Among the most difficult aspects of crisis management was explaining to Congress and the public what the Fed did and why. Bernanke tried to explain the link between the Fed's actions and Main Street, for example, through two interviews on the TV show *60 Minutes*, but the unprecedented nature of the actions compounded the problem of explanation; lending is why the Fed was founded, but it hadn't engaged in that sort or scale of crisis management in many decades. There was no precedent for the assets purchases it engaged in, allowing the imaginations of some observers to conjure up all kinds of adverse consequences that, to date, have not materialized. And transparency about some of the actions—for example, who took its loans—could run counter to the efficacy of the policy. Public misunderstanding was widespread and echoed (and amplified) in the Congress. The Federal Reserve was perceived to be bailing out large banks and Wall Street more generally, sometimes perceived to be at the expense of Main Street. On monetary policy, it was arguing the counterfactual—it would have been worse without its actions.

Despite the difficulties of explication and understanding, evidence and analysis strongly support the conclusion that the Federal Reserve's actions limited the damage to jobs and income from plunging real estate prices and expedited the return to the agency's objective of "maximum employment and stable prices."

5
Fiscal Policy and Full Employment

Laurence Ball
Johns Hopkins University

J. Bradford DeLong
University of California–Berkeley

Lawrence H. Summers
Harvard University

At present and going forward, activist fiscal policy is likely to be essential for the U.S. economy to operate near potential levels of output and employment. This view is a substantial departure from the near-consensus of economists that monetary policy alone could and should be left to carry out the stabilization policy mission, a belief that prevailed for nearly a generation prior to the 2008 financial crisis.

As of 2007, the "Great Moderation" in the United States had lasted for 20 years (see Stock and Watson [2003]). Since 1984, fluctuations in output and unemployment had been modest and seemed to even out over time, and confidence grew that the business cycle had been largely tamed. Much of the credit for this experience went to monetary policy, which had learned how to coarsely tune if not fine-tune the economy. In 1997, it was Paul Krugman who said, "the unemployment rate will be what Alan Greenspan wants it to be, plus or minus a random error reflecting the fact that he is not quite God" (Krugman 1997). The Federal Reserve appeared to have the tools to successfully manage aggregate demand to achieve the maximum levels of employment and production consistent with rough price stability.

Ten years ago, most economists likewise agreed that fiscal policy should *not* be a tool for smoothing the business cycle. Instead, the focus of good fiscal policy was the right-sizing of government spending and the control of budget deficits. Preventing excessive deficits was essential to maintaining confidence and avoiding unduly high interest rates that would slow economic growth. Adding an unnecessary stabilization policy mission to fiscal policy, so the near-consensus went, could only create distraction and confusion to no benefit.

But in 2008 the Great Moderation came to an abrupt close, as the financial crisis that began a year earlier ushered in the Great Recession. On December 5, 2008, the Federal Reserve lowered the federal funds rate below 20 basis points (0.2 percent), using up all its conventional monetary policy ammunition. Since then, the Fed has sought to boost aggregate demand through the unconventional policies of forward guidance and quantitative easing. Yet despite this monetary stimulus, the recovery that technically began in the second half of 2009 has been dismal in regard to moving output and employment toward their pre-2008 trends, and also in comparison with previous recoveries from deep recessions.

In some ways, the end of the Great Moderation and the onset of the Great Recession have had remarkably little impact on public policy debates. The most discussed economic issue in Washington over the last four years has been the need for strong action to achieve fiscal consolidation, not the urgency to restore full employment. Even though inflation and employment are both well below target, the vast majority of criticism directed at the Fed has been that its policy is too lax.

One change in public discourse, however, has been a shift from the optimism of the Great Moderation to a growing belief that the damage to the labor force and economy from the Great Recession is permanent, and that we are settling into a "new normal" in which employment levels easily reached before 2008 are now unattainable.

Although the new economic conditions of the post–Great Moderation era do require substantially new economic thinking, they do not warrant an attitude of resignation about a semi-stagnant new normal. Ironically, the appropriate new thinking is largely old thinking: traditional Keynesian ideas of the 1930s–1960s that were largely downplayed in the wake of the stagflation of the 1970s and the accompanying "New Classical" revolution in macroeconomic theory. Three concepts comprise the most important of these ideas: 1) Keynes's view that the liquidity trap, or zero bound on short-term nominal interest rates, can sharply limit the efficacy of monetary stabilization policy; 2) President John F. Kennedy's "Economics 101" view of the desirability of fiscal stimulus during a slump; and 3) the possibility that a prolonged episode of weak demand and high unemployment in an economy may have destructive consequences for aggregate supply (Blanchard and Summers 1986; Okun 1973).

After outlining these ideas, we discuss policy implications. In an economy with a depressed labor market and monetary policy constrained by the zero bound, there is a strong case for a fiscal expansion to boost aggregate demand. The benefits from such a policy greatly exceed traditional estimates of fiscal multipliers, both because increases in demand raise expected inflation, which reduces real interest rates, and because pushing the economy toward full employment will have long-lasting positive effects on the labor force and productivity.

We argue that in a liquidity trap environment like the one we are experiencing at present, properly designed fiscal stimulus is likely to reduce rather than increase the long-run debt burden.[1] This outcome reflects a combination of the direct benefits of stimulus in raising revenues; the favorable impact of increased gross domestic product in reducing the debt/GDP ratio; the possibility that fiscal stimulus today reduces future spending burdens, such as the cost of deferred maintenance; favorable supply impacts of public investments; and possible reductions in real interest rate costs that come from increases in expected inflation.

We also present new evidence derived from recent research at the Federal Reserve. Reifschneider, Wascher, and Wilcox (2013) introduce *hysteresis* on the supply side into the Federal Reserve's principal macroeconomic model. Hysteresis refers to a situation in which cyclical economic downturns diminish the economy's ability to produce output in the future. The finding from this exercise is that a sustained increase in government purchases can reduce the long-run debt/GDP ratio, even in the absence of direct supply-side benefits from government purchases, and even in the absence of any impact of current purchases on future needs for government spending.

THE DOWNTURN AND THE DISAPPOINTING RECOVERY

Figure 5.1, from Reifschneider, Wascher, and Wilcox (2013), traces the behavior of real GDP (the bottom line) relative to the supply-side

Figure 5.1 Federal Reserve Estimates of Potential Output

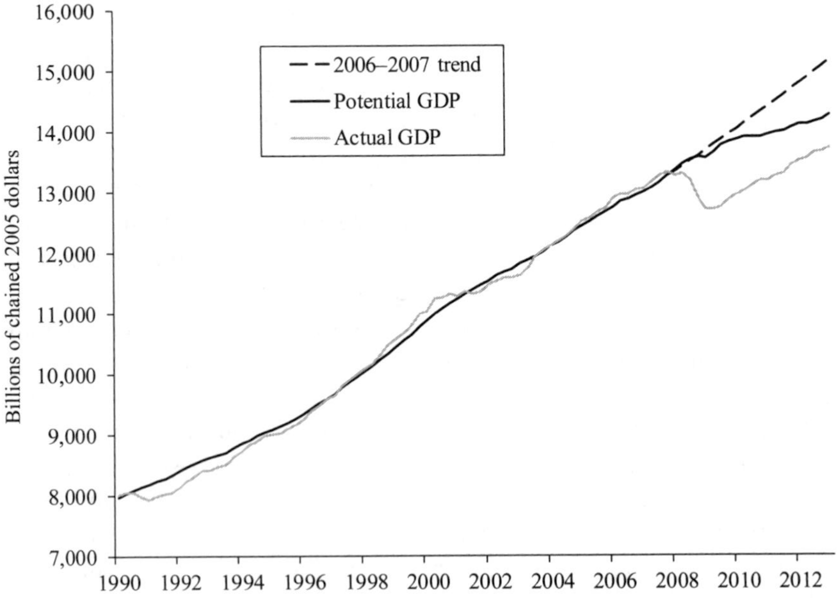

SOURCE: Reifschneider, Wascher, and Wilcox (2013).

growth trend that the economy appeared to be following before 2008, as estimated by the authors' state-space model from pre–financial crisis data (the top line). In 2013 GDP was approximately 10 percent below its previous trend, with output growing too slowly to close this gap. (The middle line in the graph is the Fed's statistical estimate of how much of the output loss is permanent, a major focus of what follows.)

Similarly, it appears that only very limited progress has been made in returning employment to normal levels. While unemployment has declined substantially, from its peak of 10.0 percent in October 2009 to 6.7 percent in February 2014, this 3.3 percentage point decline is mostly a reflection of labor force withdrawal rather than successful job finding. The fall in the official unemployment rate has not been accompanied by the 1.0 percentage point rise in labor force participation that one would expect based on past recoveries, but rather by a further 2.0 point decline. Thus, arithmetically, only 0.3 points of the decline in the unemployment rate are due to increases in the employment-to-population ratio, and 3.0 points are due to dropouts from the labor force.[2]

The employment-to-population ratio peaked at 63.4 percent in December 2006, fell sharply to 58.5 percent in October 2009, and since then has flatlined, standing today at 58.8 percent. Of particular concern are the persistently high rates of long-term unemployment, defined as the share of the labor force looking for work for at least six months. Since 1975, the average long-term jobless rate has been about 1.0 percent, but over the last downturn it peaked at a historically unprecedented level of 4.4 percent, and it remains highly elevated at over 2.0 percent.

This erosion of labor force participation and of estimates of potential output since 2007 has no obvious cause related to factor supply or technology. Indeed, it has come as a surprise to nearly all forecasters. The Congressional Budget Office's (CBO) forecasts of potential output as of 2008 included no future growth slowdown. In January 2010, CBO projected an average unemployment rate for 2013 of 6.2 percent; the actual rate was 7.3 percent. CBO projected a labor force participation rate of 65.1 percent for 2014; actual labor force participation in February 2014 was 63.0 percent.

If we look at history, we can see why economists expected a strong recovery from the Great Recession, and we can see why it did not happen. The worst post–World War II recession before that of 2008–2009 was the recession of 1981–1982. The unemployment rate peaked at 10.8 percent at the end of 1982 but then fell rapidly to 7.2 percent with rising labor force participation over the following year and a half. Unemployment was pushed down rapidly by output growth rates of 7–8 percent. With that experience as background, it was not unnatural to anticipate as of late 2009 a similar recovery from the spike in unemployment.

This expectation, however, neglected to consider the reasons for the 1980s recovery. As documented by Romer and Romer (1994), rapid growth after 1982 was fueled by the countercyclical policy of the Federal Reserve. With short-term nominal interest rates at 15 percent when the 1980s downturn began, the Fed had ample room to reduce interest rates sharply and continue to reduce them until a strong recovery took hold. The Fed also reduced interest rates in 2008, but the loosening cycle began with the federal funds rate at 5 percent, and by the end of that year the funds rate had already hit its lower bound of zero—just as economists such as Rudebusch (2009) were estimating that, according to standard interest rate rules, the economy needed rates of −4 or −5 percent for a strong recovery. Such a degree of monetary ease was obviously impossible: nobody would lend money at a significantly negative nominal interest rate rather than hold currency.

The idea that interest rates can get stuck above the level needed for full employment, constraining the effectiveness of monetary policy, is the liquidity trap that Keynes (1936) emphasized in his General Theory. Through most of the decades since Keynes wrote, the liquidity trap was considered a theoretical oddity of little practical importance—a concept useful primarily for designing trick questions on college economics exams. But U.S. short-term nominal interest rates on safe assets like government securities have been stuck at zero for more than five years. Japanese short-term safe rates have been below 1 percent for 20 years. An escape from the liquidity trap is not imminent. The median FOMC participant is now anticipating that as of December 2015 the federal funds rate will still be only 75 basis points (0.75 percent). And at every stage since 2007, the median FOMC participant has overestimated the future strength of the economy, the level of inflation, and the level of interest rates. The futures market is more pessimistic, predicting a December 2015 federal funds rate of 60 basis points.

The Fed certainly still has some expansionary policy options. Even when the federal funds rate is constrained by the zero bound, the Fed can still lower longer-term interest rates by providing forward guidance as to the future path of the short-term rate, and via "quantitative easing." However, as even strong proponents recognize, quantitative easing policies raise issues of sustainability, market distortion, efficacy, and exit management. Moreover, the experience of both the United States and the United Kingdom over the last year raises doubts about the credibility of long-term forward guidance.

As DeLong and Summers (2012) explain at length, the liquidity trap magnifies the impact of fiscal policy on economic activity and employment. During a liquidity trap, interest rates will not increase when a fiscal expansion raises the level of demand, thereby avoiding the crowding-out effects that normally arise from fiscal policies. Moreover, with a fixed nominal interest rate, if increases in demand raise the rate of inflation, real interest rates fall and investment is stimulated.

This last point deserves emphasis. In normal times, the Federal Reserve has a preferred level of economic activity given its views on output and employment; it therefore can be expected to offset any fiscal impacts on growth. This was the logic behind the Clinton 1993 budget program. Reducing prospective deficits was expected to and in fact did lead to a reduction in interest rates, which in turn crowded in investment, stimulating growth.

Under current circumstances, though, fiscal stimulus crowds in investment to the extent that it succeeds in raising future demand and therefore profit levels, and to the extent that it succeeds in raising expected future inflation and thus reduces real interest rates.

THE LONG-TERM EFFECTS OF CYCLICAL SLUMPS

Evidence from Historical Comparisons and Labor Market Studies

The lessons of economic history suggest that the tepid quality of the current U.S. recovery should not be too surprising. For ease of presentation, economics textbooks typically portray recessions as temporary events, as part of a "cycle" that is independent of and does not affect the longer-run "trend," and after a recession, losses in output and employment are reversed within a few years. But empirical support for this view comes primarily from the United States between 1873 and 1970 and is complicated by the fact that the Great Depression of the 1930s was followed by the countervailing extraordinary war mobilization of World War II. The textbook model of short-term recessions is contradicted by research based on broader international data. International Monetary Fund (IMF) studies, such as the *2009 World Economic Outlook* (IMF 2009) that look at post–World War II financial crises, find that essentially *all* of the output decline associated with a typical crisis persists for at least seven years, and little or none of the shortfall relative to the precrisis trend is recovered within that time span. Reinhart and Rogoff (2009) and others have also documented that the output losses following financial crises are persistent indeed. The ugly technical term for these highly persistent effects is hysteresis.

Earlier work such as Blanchard and Summers (1986) as well as Ball (1999) focused on the effects of deep recessions on the natural rate of unemployment. The empirical record showed that increases in unemployment often were highly persistent. In many European countries, the recessions in the 1980s and 1990s caused rises in unemployment that were never reversed, and unemployment ratcheted up again as the 2008 crisis spread around the world. There appeared to be a correlation between persistent unemployment-rate increases after a downturn and an absence of a strong stimulative monetary response to recession. Although the zero bound on interest rates was rarely binding, monetary policy was constrained by other factors. Often the key factor was either Europe's current common currency or the system of fixed exchange rates that preceded it. Sometimes countercyclical monetary policy was precluded by anti-inflationary zeal on the part of policymakers, notably Margaret Thatcher in the United Kingdom. The absence of sufficient monetary stimulus is a feature that these episodes have in common with the recent U.S. experience, as the appropriate monetary policy response, at least in the interest-rate-rule calculations of Rudebusch, was mathematically impossible.

The historical evidence for hysteresis is complemented by lines of research in labor economics by Davis and von Wachter (2011); Ghyrad (2013); Oreopoulos, von Wachter, and Heisz (2012); and many others. This work documents substantial deleterious effects of deep economic slumps on individual workers who lose jobs—in other words, the microeconomic problems that underlie persistent unemployment. Lost jobs disrupt careers because workers become less and less likely to find new jobs as the length of their unemployment spells increases. An experiment by Ghyrad, in which resumes were sent to employers that advertised jobs, finds that workers with more than six months of unemployment experienced very low employer response rates—lower than those for workers who had less relevant experience but did not possess the stigma of a long unemployment spell.

Even when an unemployed worker finds a job, it is typically lower paying than the worker's previous job. It is striking that this adverse effect on earnings is still apparent decades later.

It is even more striking, as Davis and von Wachter (2011) find, that these effects are particularly large when a worker loses a job during a recession. A rational-signaling model in which a long unemployment spell reveals that a worker is potentially of a low-productivity type would imply that those who lose their jobs due to an aggregate shock like a financial crisis are more likely than other unemployed workers to reattain employment.

As Oreopoulos, von Wachter, and Heisz (2012) find, a recession also damages the long-term prospects of young workers entering the labor force. Those who graduate from college during a recession have worse labor market prospects. Once again, the adverse effects on workers' earnings last for decades.

Evidence from Federal Reserve Staff Estimates

These harmful effects on individual workers are not the only long-term damage from recessions. As emphasized by Reifschneider, Wascher, and Wilcox (2013), physical investment falls sharply in recessions. The pace at which new firms are formed also falls, as does research and development by existing firms and the development and testing of business models. Distortions of the economy's relative price structure and the shortfall in spending initiated by a recession make it difficult to do the economic calculation of whether an investment project is profitable. All of these effects make for a less-productive economy in the long term.

Reifschneider, Wascher, and Wilcox (2013) currently estimate that three-tenths of the 10 percent shortfall of U.S. output relative to the pre-2008 trend will eventually be reversed but that the rest is a permanent downward-level shift in the path of potential output. Today's level of potential output appears to be roughly 7 percent lower than the level anticipated before the 2008 crisis.

Evidence from the Congressional Budget Office Assessment of Potential Output

The Federal Reserve staff assessments of the long-run shadow cast on potential output by the Great Recession are consistent with current analysis by the Congressional Budget Office. As the weak recovery has dragged on, CBO has reduced its forecasts of potential output. The forecast for 2014 made in 2013 is 8.2 percent lower than the forecast for 2014 made in 2007. Yang (2014) has decomposed this loss of potential output into three components. He finds that about 40 percent is explained by a long-term decline in projected future labor input measured by total hours worked, 50 percent is explained by a decline in investment and thus in the accumulation path of physical capital, and the remaining 10 percent is explained by a fall in the projected growth path of total factor productivity.

A CBO (2014) study suggests that the Great Recession is not the reason that potential output has fallen below the path the agency forecast before 2008. "The impact of cyclical weakness in the economy accounts for just 1.8 percentage points, or about one-fourth, of the difference from the 2007 projection, even though the downward revision to potential GDP coincided with the severe recession of 2007–2009 and the subsequent slow recovery" (p. 2). The report states that the primary reason it has reduced its forecasts of potential output is a slowdown in trend output growth that began early in the 2000s—but which the agency's researchers only detected recently—and it is a coincidence that this pre-2007 growth slowdown was only recognized in the aftermath of the Great Recession.

We remain skeptical of CBO's view. As we noted, research consistently finds that recessions following financial crises cause long-term losses in output. The disappointing U.S. growth since 2007 fits this pattern. It is natural to interpret recent experience as a typical example of hysteresis, not as some more subtle shift in the economy unrelated to the recession that occurred at the same time.

Moreover, CBO's position does not appear fully consistent with Figure 5.2, which depicts the evolution of CBO's estimate of potential 2014 GDP. It is noteworthy that the potential output path declines steadily from 2007 to 2014. This pattern appears contrary to the CBO claim that revisions are explained by slow growth before 2007 and the fact that 2007 was a cyclical peak. If those were the real sources of the revisions, they should have been heavily frontloaded relative to the downturn—in other words, most of CBO's revisions should have occurred as soon as it recognized 2007 as a peak (the National Bureau of Economic Research called it in December 2008). This is not the case.

As CBO discusses in its 2014 report, its current estimates of potential output growth are heavily influenced by actual output growth between 2001 and 2007, the last two cyclical peaks. A problem with this approach is that 2001 was a very strong peak—output appears to

Figure 5.2 Estimates of 2014 Potential GDP, at Different Points in Time

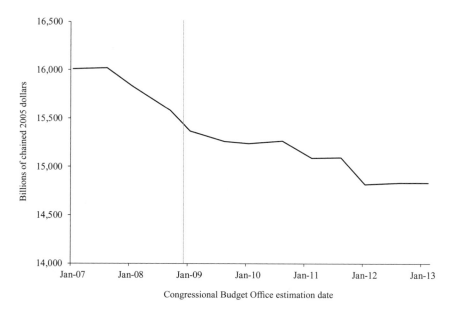

Congressional Budget Office estimation date

NOTE: Vertical line: In December 2008, the National Bureau of Economic Research announced December 2007 as a business cycle peak.
SOURCE: Analysis of Congressional Budget Office data by Yang (2014).

have risen substantially above potential, as reflected by the unemployment rate of 3.9 percent in late 2000. The 2007 peak was a weak one—it achieved its status as a peak only because growth was halted abruptly by the financial crisis. We suspect that the growth of output between a strong peak and a weak peak—from a point well above potential to one closer to potential—underestimates the trend growth rate.

THE POTENTIAL FOR RECOVERY

The U.S. economy is on a path toward long-term underperformance, but this outcome is not inevitable. The economy spiraled downward in 2008 because of a fall in aggregate demand—sharp declines in consumption and investment resulting from the disruption of the financial system and accompanying panic. We believe that a sufficient strengthening of demand can push output back toward its pre-2008 trend and minimize the long-term damage from the Great Recession.

Where might stronger aggregate demand come from? We can hope for good luck, such as a surge in investment in new technologies, a rise in exports driven by economic growth in other countries, or a return to normal levels of risk tolerance on the part of savers and financial intermediaries. But a more reliable approach is to use macroeconomic policy to boost demand.

During the Great Moderation era before 2008, macroeconomic policy typically meant monetary policy. In today's weak economy, the Federal Reserve should certainly try to support aggregate demand through an accommodative policy stance. Economists are actively debating how much unconventional monetary policies such as quantitative easing have contributed to the recovery, the potential for further unconventional policies going forward, and whatever risks might be created by the interaction of a very large Federal Reserve balance sheet and our current banking and regulatory system. We will not take a position on these complex and unsettled issues. Instead, we will emphasize the most straightforward way to stimulate demand at the zero bound: fiscal expansion.

A Role for Fiscal Policy?

Fiscal expansion could take the form of cuts in net taxes or increases in government spending. Well-targeted policies such as public investment would have important direct benefits because the United States has systematically underinvested in public infrastructure capital. But for the current discussion the key effect of fiscal policy is the boost that it provides to aggregate demand.

There have been many conflicting claims in the public debate about the effects of fiscal policy. Many argue that fiscal expansion is counterproductive because it reduces economic confidence and thus private spending by more than it increases public spending. However, there has now been enough policy experience and research to reach a clear and firm conclusion: fiscal expansion is indeed expansionary in economies like the United States today, where interest rates are near the zero bound and therefore there is little risk of crowding out private investment. Several years ago, after reviewing a variety of evidence, including cross-country and time-series analysis and micro examinations of the 2009 Obama stimulus, David Romer (2011) concluded that the positive effects of fiscal expansion are an issue "that we should view as settled." Since then, Blanchard and Leigh (2013) have found that fiscal multipliers in advanced economies were larger than expected during 2009 and 2010, with the result that output fell short of IMF forecasts in countries that pursued fiscal austerity. Under current conditions, the multiplier—the effect of a dollar of spending or of net tax cuts on GDP—appears likely to be not just positive but greater than 1.0.

An economy with a positive multiplier, with hysteresis, and with interest rates on short-term government debt at their zero bound has very different characteristics from what we used to think of as a normal economy—one with interest rates even on short-term Treasury debt bounded well away from zero, with monetary offsets to fiscal policy substantially reducing if not eliminating the multiplier, and with a tendency to rapidly return to a predownturn potential growth path. In what we used to see as a normal economy, a fiscal boost had little effect on current employment and production and, because it raised the debt/GDP ratio, induced substantial future drag on potential output through its amortization costs. But when interest rates are near zero, amortization costs are near or less than zero, monetary policy offset is absent, and persistent hysteresis effects on the tax base have a very high present value. In this setting, a sizable fiscal expansion could go a long way toward restoring full employment. A shift to greater austerity would have the opposite effects. Either way, decisions about fiscal policy today will influence the economy into the distant future.

Fiscal Policy and Debt in the Long Run

Our advocacy of a fiscal expansion runs strongly counter to the conventional wisdom, which is that long-run fiscal sustainability requires that the government tighten its belt in response to a downturn that reduces the tax base, even—or perhaps especially—in the case of hysteresis. At a time when the government's net debt has risen above 70 percent of a year's GDP, concerns about the federal government's debt are no doubt legitimate. An increase in the debt/GDP ratio certainly has

the potential to reduce the funds available for productive private investment relative to a counterfactual with a stable debt/GDP ratio. And a
debt that is or even looks out of control is a threat to financial stability,
and via its effects on real interest rates an additional drag on capital
formation even if current debt and deficits are not that large.

It is natural to think that a cut in net taxes or an increase in government purchases increases the national debt, and indeed that is the short-
run effect. In the view of many reasonable people, that fact creates a
dilemma: a fiscal expansion is good for the unemployment problem, but
bad for the debt problem. We believe, however, that this tradeoff does
not really exist. Under current circumstances, the *long-run* effects of
fiscal expansion on the debt are benign.

This conclusion follows from the long-lasting effects of fiscal
expansion on output. In the presence of hysteresis, a one-time temporary cut in net taxes increases output into the distant future. A persistent
output increase creates a persistent rise in tax revenue. These long-term
fiscal benefits can more than amortize the initial rise in the deficit if the
real cost of financing government debt remains low enough.

DeLong and Summers (2012) analyze the conditions under which
a tax cut pays for itself. The key parameters in their analysis include
the short-run multiplier, the effect of a tax cut on current output, and
also the "degree of hysteresis," the effect of a rise in current output on
potential output, which is an effect that persists into the future. Another
key parameter is the marginal tax rate for the economy, the extra tax
revenue that accrues from an extra dollar of output. For the United
States, the marginal tax rate is approximately one-third. Together, the
multiplier, the degree of hysteresis, and the marginal tax rate determine
the long-run revenue gains from a current fiscal expansion.

Readers can consult the DeLong-Summers paper for the algebra,
which also involves the interest rate paid by the government on its debt.
The bottom line is that, for realistic values of the multiplier and the
marginal tax rate, and assuming interest rates in the future are not much
higher than in the past, only a small degree of hysteresis is needed for
a tax cut to pay for itself. A degree of hysteresis of 0.05 is more than
sufficient: this means that a $1.00 rise in current output must have an
effect on potential output of $0.05 through its effects on investment, the
labor force attachment of workers, and so on. DeLong and Summers
argue that the degree of hysteresis is likely to exceed this threshold by

a substantial margin, based on both historical evidence and the recent U.S. experience.

Calibrating the Analysis

We can use the estimates of potential output in Reifschneider, Wascher, and Wilcox (2013) to produce a simple estimate of the value of the hysteresis coefficients η. Figure 5.1 shows the Reifschneider et al. state-space model estimates of the path of the output gap γ, measured as the difference between potential output (the middle line in the figure) and actual output (the bottom line). The output gap peaked at 7.3 percent in the third quarter of 2009. Added up over time, the cumulative output gap $C(\gamma)$ through the first quarter of 2013 equaled 24.9 percentage point years of U.S. potential output.

Let σ for "scarring" or "shadow" be the difference between what potential output would have been in the first quarter of 2013 based on the pre-2008 trend and where it ended up in that quarter according to the Fed estimates. The value of σ = 6.0 percent. The implicit estimate of hysteresis η is then simply:

(5.1) $\eta = \sigma / C(\gamma)$

and so $\eta = (6.0)/(24.9) = 0.24$.

The estimate of η, 0.24, far exceeds the level of hysteresis required for a tax cut to be self-financing, which is 0.05 or less in the DeLong-Summers analysis.

A more sophisticated exercise looks more deeply into the Federal Reserve Board/U.S. (FRB/US) macroeconomic model that underpins the analysis of Reifschneider, Wascher, and Wilcox (2013) and is one of the main tools used by the Federal Reserve. The baseline model includes one hysteresis effect: a fall in output reduces physical invest-ment, which causes a long-lasting decrease in labor productivity. Rei-fschneider, Wascher, and Wilcox augment this channel with hysteresis in the labor market: an output slump has persistent effects on the unem-ployment rate and labor force participation calibrated to be "roughly consistent with the experience of the last few years."[3] In unpublished work, Reifschneider and Summers (n.d.) simulate the FRB/US model with and without labor-side hysteresis, taking as their initial conditions the state of the U.S. economy at the business cycle trough in 2009 and anticipation that the federal funds rate would remain at zero for a number of years. They derive the effects of an increase in government spending of 1 percent of GDP for six years, from 2009 through 2014. Figure 5.3 shows the simulated effects of this fiscal stimulus on output, potential output, the government deficit, and debt.

Panel A in Figure 5.3 shows how the additional fiscal expansion in 2009 causes output to rise sharply in both versions of the model. Panel B shows the corresponding rise in potential output, which is much larger in the model that includes hysteresis in the labor market. The increase in potential output leads the stimulus to have an effect on real GDP that persists even after the policy's direct effects on aggregate demand are gone.

Panels C and D in Figure 5.3 show that even in the baseline FRB/US model, the debt/GDP ratio eventually falls below the level it would have attained without the stimulus. In the model with calibrated labor-market hysteresis, the debt/GDP ratio immediately falls below and always remains below its baseline no-additional-stimulus level. Twenty years after the fiscal stimulus begins, this policy has reduced the debt/GDP ratio by 2.2 percentage points.

There is every reason to expect that these calculations are conservative. Allowing for a supply-side impact of increased public spending or the possibility that increases today would obviate the need for spending in the future, as in the case of necessary infrastructure maintenance, would augment the reduction in the debt/GDP ratio.

CONCLUSION

The weak recovery of the labor market is a national crisis with a real human dimension. The effects of job loss, in addition to financial strain, include damage to physical and mental health. Studies have linked unemployment to higher death rates, particularly immediately after job loss, but even in the long run by 10–15 percent for at least the next 20 years; higher rates of suicide as unemployment duration stretches on; and even higher rates of cancer mortality. Furthermore, studies have

**Figure 5.3   Effects of a 1 Percent of GDP Increase in Federal Purchases
for Five Years, with and without Labor-Market Hysterisis**

Panel A: Real GDP Level

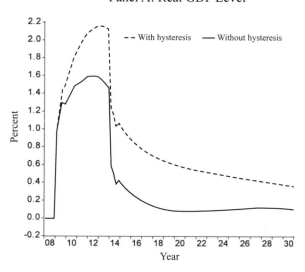

Panel B: Potential GDP Level

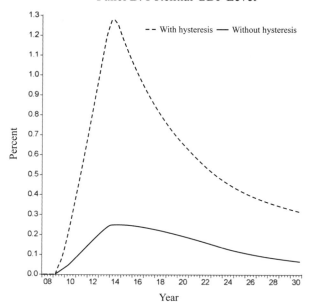

(continued)

Figure 5.3 (continued)

Panel C: Federal Surplus-to-GDP Ratio (NIA Basis)

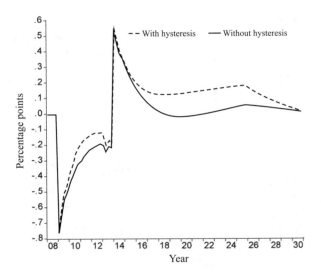

Panel D: Debt-to-GDP Ratio

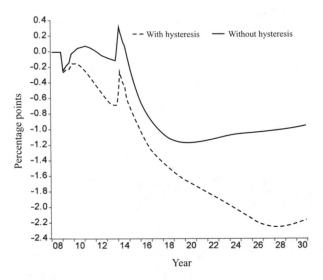

SOURCE: Reifschneider and Summers (n.d.).

found that family members of people who have lost their jobs are also affected: being laid off increases the likelihood of divorce in the years immediately following the layoff, and children of laid-off workers are around 15 percent more likely to have to repeat a grade. Furthermore, the longer one is unemployed, the harder it is to find a new job, and thus the harder it becomes to escape these terrible costs (Charles and Stephens Jr. 2001; Classen and Dunn 2012; Huff Stevens and Schaller 2009; Lynge 1997; Shimer 2008; Sullivan and von Wachter 2009).

How can policymakers restore full employment? In our view, it is easier than one might think. Economics usually teaches us not to believe in a free lunch. But with even a small degree of hysteresis in a standard economic model such as the Federal Reserve's forecasting model, fiscal policymakers face an easy decision if the economy is weak with low labor demand and if interest rates are stuck at the zero bound. A fiscal expansion is then a win-win policy. It not only raises employment and output; it also reduces the long-term problem of government debt. Conversely, an insistence on austerity in these circumstances has perverse effects: it *worsens* the debt problem that motivates the policy, it prolongs the economic slump, and it magnifies the long-term damage to the labor force and productivity. Keynes was right about fiscal policy, and Herbert Hoover was wrong about the virtues of belt-tightening during an economic slump.

This past recession will not be the nation's last, and expansionary fiscal policy will likely be needed again in the future. For reasons laid out in Summers (2013), we believe that the safe real interest rate necessary for full employment has declined considerably in the United States, raising concerns about secular stagnation—the idea that the financial conditions necessary for adequate growth and production near potential output are likely unsustainable, and that sustainable finance is likely to go along with unsatisfactory growth and production well below potential output. Under such circumstances, it is likely that the zero lower bound on interest rates will be reached more frequently in the future than in the past, that fiscal expansion will reduce the need for extraordinary monetary policies that potentially create instability, and that debt burdens are less problematic because of lower interest rates.

Notes

This paper was prepared as part of the Full Employment Project at the Center for Budget and Policy Priorities, with support from the Rockefeller Foundation.

1. This idea has a long pedigree, dating back to at least the 1940s, the last time long-term U.S. government real and nominal interest rates were this low. See Lerner (1943).
2. Some of the labor force decline is due to demography; nevertheless, Hatzius and Mericle (2014) suggest that the unemployment gap—the difference between the current rate and full employment—is at least 2.5 percentage points, and this is four and a half years into an economic expansion.
3. In the specification of Reifschneider, Wascher, and Wilcox (2013), labor market hysteresis arises when unemployment exceeds its natural rate by 1.25 percentage points or more. In this situation, an additional percentage point of unemployment in a quarter causes a persistent increase in the natural rate of 0.02 points and a persistent decrease in labor force participation of 0.04 points.

References

Ball, Laurence. 1999. "Aggregate Demand and Long-Run Unemployment." In *Brookings Papers on Economic Activity, 2*, William C. Brainard and George L. Perry, eds. Washington, DC: Brookings Institution, pp. 189–251.

Blanchard, Olivier, and Daniel Leigh. 2013. "Growth Forecast Errors and Fiscal Multipliers," International Monetary Fund Working Paper 13/1. Washington, DC: International Monetary Fund.

Blanchard, Olivier J., and Lawrence H. Summers. 1986. "Hysteresis and the European Unemployment Problem." In *NBER Macroeconomics Annual, 1986*, Stanley Fisher, ed. Cambridge, MA: MIT Press, pp. 15–90.

Charles, Kerwin Kofi, and Melvin Stephens Jr. 2001. "Job Displacement, Disability, and Divorce." NBER Working Paper No. 8578. Cambridge, MA: National Bureau of Economic Research. http://www.nber.org/papers/w8578.pdf (accessed April 4, 2017).

Classen, Timothy J., and Richard A. Dunn. 2012. "The Effect of Job Loss and Unemployment Duration on Suicide Risk in the United States: A New Look Using Mass Layoffs and Unemployment Insurance Claims." *Health Economics* 21(3): 338–350.

Congressional Budget Office. 2014. "Revisions to CBO's Projection of Potential Output Since 2007." Washington, DC: CBO. http://www.cbo.gov/sites/default/files/cbofiles/attachments/45150-PotentialOutput.pdf (accessed April 4, 2017).

Davis, Steven J., and Till von Wachter. 2012. "Recessions and the Costs of Job Loss," *Brookings Papers on Economic Activity, 2*, David H. Romer and Justin Wolfers, eds. Washington, DC: Brookings Institution, pp. 1–55.

DeLong, Bradford J., and Lawrence H. Summers. 2012. "Fiscal Policy in a Depressed Economy." In *Brookings Papers on Economic Activity, 2*, David H. Romer and Justin Wolfers, eds. Washington, DC: Brookings Institution, pp. 233–274.

Ghyrad, Rand. 2013. "The Jobless Trap." Boston, MA: Northeastern University.

Hatzius, Jan, and David Mericle. 2014. "U.S. Daily: A Roundup on Labor Market Slack and Wages." Goldman Sachs Research, February 14.

International Monetary Fund. 2009. "What's the Damage: Medium-Term Output Dynamics After Financial Crises." *World Economic Outlook*. Washington, DC: IMF, pp. 121–151.

Keynes, John Maynard. 1936. *The General Theory of Employment, Interest, and Money*. London: Macmillan and Co.

Krugman, Paul. 1997. "Vulgar Keynesians." *Slate*, February 6. http://web.mit.edu/krugman/www/vulgar.html (accessed April 4, 2017).

Lerner, Abba. 1943. "Functional Finance and the Federal Debt." *Social Research* 10(1): 38–51.

Lynge, E. 1997. "Unemployment and Cancer: A Literature Review." In *Social Inequalities and Cancer*, Manolis Kogevinas, Neil Pearce, Mervyn Susser, and P. Boffetta, eds. IARC Scientific Publication No. 138. Lyon, France: International Agency for Research on Cancer, pp. 343–351. http://www.iarc.fr/en/publications/pdfs-online/epi/sp138/sp138-chap16.pdf (accessed April 4, 2017).

Okun, Arthur M. 1973. "Upward Mobility in a High-Pressure Economy." *Brookings Papers on Economic Activity* 1: 207–261.

Oreopoulos, Phillip, Till von Wachter, and Andrew Heisz. 2012. "The Short- and Long-Term Career Effects of Graduating in a Recession." *American Economic Journal: Applied Economics* 4(1): 1–29.

Reifschneider, Dave, and Larry Summers. n.d. Unpublished work from ongoing analysis.

Reifschneider, Dave, William Wascher, and David Wilcox. 2013. "Aggregate Supply in the United States: Recent Developments and Implications for the Conduct of Monetary Policy." FEDS Working Paper 2013-77. Washington, DC: Federal Reserve Board.

Reinhart, Carmen M., and Kenneth S. Rogoff. 2009. "The Aftermath of Financial Crises." *American Economic Review* 99(2): 466–472).

Romer, Christina, and David Romer. 1994. "What Ends Recessions?" In *NBER Macroeconomics Annual, 1994*, Stanley Fisher and Julio J. Rotemberg, eds. Cambridge, MA: MIT Press, pp. 13–57.

Romer, David. 2011. "What Have We Learned About Fiscal Policy From the Crisis?" Paper presented at the International Monetary Fund "Conference on Macro and Growth Policies in the Wake of the Crisis," held in Washington, DC, March 7–8.

Rudebusch, Glenn D. 2009. "The Fed's Monetary Policy Response to the Current Crisis." FRBSF Economic Letter 2009-17. San Francisco: Federal Reserve Bank of San Francisco.

Shimer, Robert. 2008. "The Probability of Finding a Job." *American Economic Review* 98(2): 268–273.

Stevens, Ann Huff, and Jessamyn Schaller. 2009. "Short-Run Effects of Parental Job Loss on Children's Academic Achievement." NBER Working Paper No. 15480. Cambridge, MA: National Bureau of Economic Research. http://www.nber.org/papers/w15480.pdf (accessed April 4, 2017).

Stock, James H., and Mark W. Watson. 2003. "Has the Business Cycle Changed and Why?" *NBER Macroeconomics Annual, 2002*, Mark Gertler and Kenneth Rogoff, eds. Cambridge, MA: MIT Press, pp. 159–218. http://www.nber.org/chapters/c11075 (accessed April 4, 2017).

Sullivan, Daniel, and Till von Wachter. 2009. "Job Displacement and Mortality: An Analysis Using Administrative Data." *Quarterly Journal of Economics* 124(3): 1265–1306.

Summers, Lawrence H. 2013. Transcript of speech at the IMF Economic Forum, held in Washington, DC, Nov. 18, 2013. https://m.facebook.com/notes/randy-fellmy/transcript-of-larry-summers-speech-at-the-imf-economic-forum-nov-8-2013/585630634864563 (accessed April 14, 2017).

Yang, David. 2014. Unpublished paper, Harvard University.

6

International Dimensions
of the Great Recession
and the Weak Recovery

Kathryn M.E. Dominguez
University of Michigan and NBER

The global economic slowdown that followed the U.S. financial crisis in 2008 was deeper and longer lasting than any previous economic downturn other than the Great Depression. Indeed, the downturn is widely referred to as the Great Recession, testimony to its severity in comparison to other postwar recessions, while at the same time delineating it as a recession and not a depression. Worldwide GDP fell by over 15 percent during the Great Depression. The global GDP decline during the Great Recession was much lower—around 1 percent—but the slow pace of the recovery from the recent downturn is unprecedented. This chapter will examine the reasons for the weak recovery from the Great Recession. Reinhart and Rogoff (2011, 2014) make a strong case for why recessions precipitated by financial crises are likely to be more severe than those caused by other factors, which is undoubtedly part of the explanation.[1] The international dimensions of the recent financial crisis are also significant contributors to both the diffusion and persistence of the weak recovery.

COMPARISONS TO THE GREAT DEPRESSION

The Great Depression started with major economic contractions in the period 1930–1933, but the U.S. economy rebounded strongly in the subsequent three years with an average growth rate of 11 percent. In contrast, the Great Recession only lasted six quarters, but growth rates have only averaged 2.2 percent over the six subsequent years. Figure 6.1 compares annual real GDP growth in the United States during the 1930s to current growth rates. It dramatically illustrates that the depth of the Great Depression far exceeded our recent experience, while at the same time showing the relatively slow pace of the current recovery.

Economists have long studied the causes and consequences of the Great Depression, and among the many lessons learned from that experience was that fiscal and monetary policy decisions in that time period likely exacerbated the severity and persistence of the downturn (Brown 1956; Friedman and Schwartz 1963; Keynes 1936; Romer 1992; Temin 1989). Figures 6.2 and 6.3 compare the fiscal and monetary policy responses taken during the Great Depression relative to actions taken in the wake of the Great Recession. As DeLong (1998) describes, the U.S. government did not consider economic stabilization, let alone full employment, as one of its responsibilities prior to the Great Depres-

Figure 6.1 Comparing the Great Recession to the Great Depression, in Annual Real GDP Growth

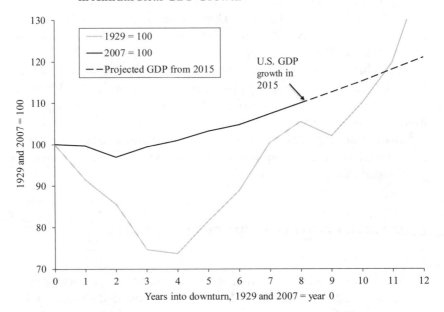

SOURCE: US. Bureau of Economic Analysis: Real GDP, not seasonally adjusted, billions of chained 2009 dollars.

Figure 6.2 U.S. Fiscal Policy Response Comparison

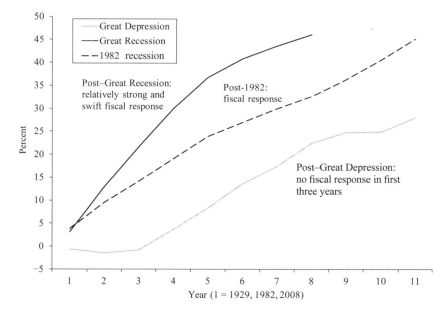

SOURCE: Federal Reserve Bank of St. Louis, US. Office of Management and Budget: Federal surplus or deficit [-] as percent of GDP (FYFSGDA188S) was first constructed by the Federal Reserve Bank of St. Louis in October 2012. It is calculated using Federal Surplus or Deficit [-] (FYFSD) and GDP (GDPA): FYFSGDA188S = [(FYFSD/1000) ÷ GDPA] × 100 FYFSD ÷ 1000.

sion. The government borrowed to pay for wars and attempted to run surpluses during peacetimes to pay off the accrued debts, which led to the principle that the only good peacetime budget was a balanced budget. It was not until the passage of the Employment Act of 1946 that the federal government was required to actively manage the macro economy, though by 1931 U.S. fiscal deficits started to rise as a consequence of the congressional override of Hoover's veto of the veterans' bonus (Hausman 2016) and other relief expenditures, as well as the collapse in tax revenues. The fiscal response to the Great Recession was, in comparative terms, strong and swift. Figure 6.2 also shows the fiscal response to the recession in 1982, which was far stronger than was the case in the 1930s but less aggressive than the approach taken after 2008. The American Recovery and Reinvestment Act (ARRA) of

Figure 6.3 U.S. Monetary Policy Response Comparison

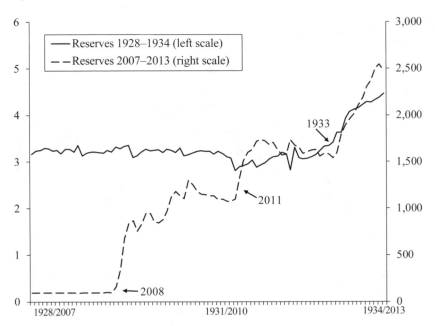

SOURCE: Federal Reserve Bank of St. Louis; St. Louis Monthly Reserves and Monetary Base.

2009 provided around $800 billion in tax cuts and federal spending to stimulate the economy, and various other programs (Cash for Clunkers, the extension and expansion of the housing tax credit, the job tax credit, and extensions of emergency unemployment insurance benefits) added another $200 billion in stimulus spending.

The U.S. monetary response to the Great Recession was also dramatically different from the approach taken in the 1930s. As is evident in Figure 6.3, it was not until the United States left the gold standard in 1933 that monetary policy became more expansionary during the Great Depression. In contrast, the Federal Reserve's immediate and unprecedented approach to providing liquidity to financial markets began with a half-point reduction in the federal funds target rate (to 4.75 percent) in September 2007, followed by further reductions that brought the target rate down to a range of 0 to 0.25 percent by December 2008. In 2007, the Fed created a Term Auction Facility (TAF), which provided banks with additional access to liquidity. This was followed by a series of extraordinary credit mechanisms: in March 2008, the Term Securities Lending Facility (TSLF), which allowed banks and eventually non-bank financial institutions to exchange less-liquid securities for U.S. Treasury bills; the Commercial Paper Funding facility; and the Term Asset-Backed Securities Loan Facility (TALF). In October 2008, the Emergency Economic Stabilization Act of 2008 was passed, which provided up to $700 billion to the Fed to purchase a wide array of illiquid assets through the Troubled Assets Relief Program (TARP). In 2009 the Fed announced its first round of quantitative easing, which involved the purchase of $1 trillion of securities, and in 2010 it announced a second round of $750 billion.

The aggressive U.S. policy response to the financial crisis was, and remains, controversial. The efficacy of specific policies, the size of the programs, and the approach to implementation will likely be debated for decades to come. Lessons from the Great Depression clearly spurred policymakers to action, and it seems likely that the policies, at the very least, delayed the slowdown in U.S. growth. However, fiscal and monetary policy actions, whether because they were not aggressive enough or because other factors complicated their efficacy, were not able to head off the Great Recession.

FORECASTING THE GREAT RECESSION

Are major economic downturns predictable? Dominguez, Fair, and Shapiro (1988) find no evidence that contemporary forecasters realized that a major economic downturn would follow the 1929 stock market crash. Likewise, there is little evidence that professional or government forecasters could predict the Great Recession. Figure 6.4 shows the probability distributions of U.S. GDP growth calculated by the Federal Reserve Bank of New York before and after the Lehman Bank failure in September 2008. The solid line in the figure is based on data available up to November 2008, and the dashed line is based on data available through April 2008. The actual depth of the Great Recession was 5 percent; in April 2008 the Fed forecasters attributed less than 3 percent

Figure 6.4   Forecasting the Great Recession: Probability Distribution before and after the Lehman Failure

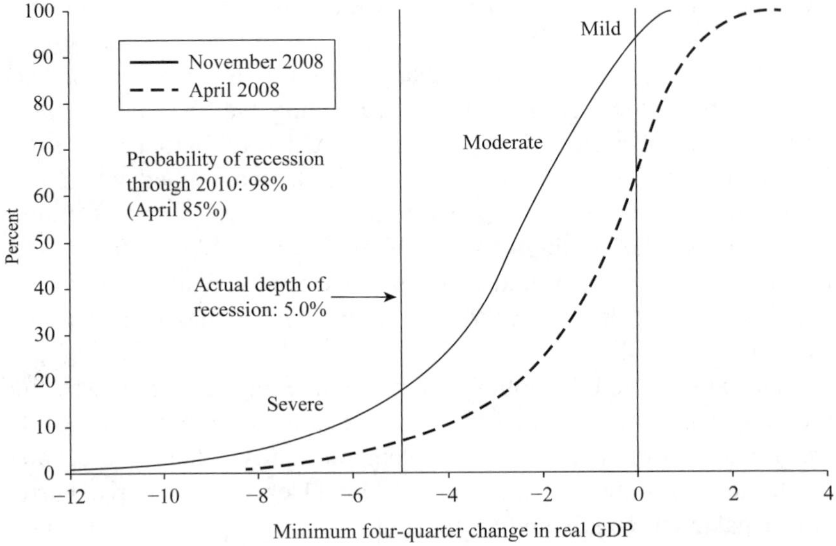

NOTE: Figure shows probability distribution of GDP growth from a calibration exercise before and after the Lehman failure. The solid line corresponds to a November 20, 2008, calibration (and therefore after Lehman) based on a 97% probability of recession (even in November 2008 the simulation had some paths that did not produce a recession), whereas the dashed line is based on a beginning of April 2008 calibration. As can be seen the shape of the conditional cumulative distribution function also changes as more weight is placed on extreme scenarios in the underlying Markov process and the fat tail of the extreme scenarios is increased. The actual depth of the 2007–2009 recession was −5% (using the pre-2013 benchmark data). As gauged by this metric, the April 2008 calibration attributed less than 3% probability to the ultimate outcome, and it was only by November 2008 that the probability of the actual outcome was close to 15%.

SOURCE: Federal Reserve Bank of New York research staff; Potter (2011).

probability to this outcome, and even in November 2008 the probability of the actual outcome was only 15 percent.

It was not just forecasts of the U.S. economy that missed the mark—there is little cross-country evidence that forecasters could predict the global downturn. Figure 6.5 shows the International Monetary Fund's (IMF) average rolling forecast errors over various horizons starting in 1990 and ending in 2012 for 188 countries. Forecast errors were gen-

Figure 6.5 IMF's Rolling Forecast Errors by Horizon, 1990–2012 (percentage points, annual average)

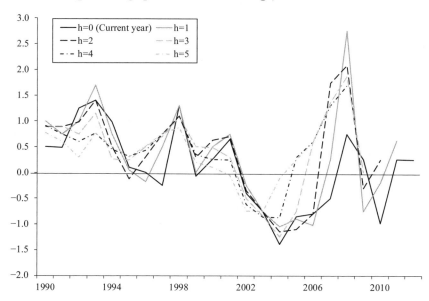

NOTE: Forecast error = forecast − actual. Actual data as of December 2013; forecasts for 0-to 5-year horizons; 188 countries.
SOURCE: IMF's World Economic Outlook (1990–2012 vintages); Figure 12 in Ho and Mauro (2014).

erally positive in the 1990s, meaning that the IMF forecast exceeded actual GDP growth. Between 2000 and 2007 forecast errors were negative, indicating that economic growth was stronger than what IMF forecasters expected. In the aftermath of the financial crisis in 2008, forecast errors again swung positive, with five-year horizon forecast errors nearing an unprecedented 3 percent.

FORECASTING THE RECOVERY

Although most forecasters missed the depth and severity of the Great Recession, they seem to have largely anticipated the slow recovery. Dominguez and Shapiro (2013) examine real GDP forecasts and forecast revisions starting in 2009 by the Survey of Professional Forecasters (SPF) maintained by the Philadelphia Fed, the Eurozone Survey of Professional Forecasters maintained by the European Central Bank (ECB), and the IMF World Economic Outlook forecasts. Figure 6.6 shows actual real U.S. GDP from 2007 to 2012 (the solid line) along with average eight-quarter-ahead SPF forecasts (the dashed lines) starting at the trough of the Great Recession (mid-2009). The SPF forecasts are initially overly pessimistic, but over time they track actual GDP growth closely, and revisions of the outlook consistently shift downward over time. In 2012 the SPF forecasts predict a downward shift not

Figure 6.6 U.S. Real GDP Forecast: Actual and Survey of Professional Forecasters, 2007–2014

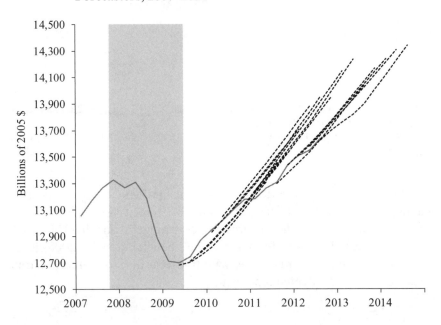

NOTE: Real GDP, billions of chained 2005 dollars, quarterly, seasonally adjusted (solid line), real-time mean eight-quarter ahead Survey of Professional Forecasters as calculated in Dominguez and Shapiro (2013) (dashed lines). The shaded area indicates the dates of the Great Recession as determined by the NBER.
SOURCE: Dominguez and Shapiro (2013, Figure 1). Federal Reserve Bank of St. Louis.

only of the trend path but also in the growth rate of GDP. Importantly, as Dominguez and Shapiro (2013) emphasize: "Nowhere in the forecast horizon since the 2009 trough have forecasters projected a return to the pre–Great Recession trend path" (pp. 149). Figure 6.7 shows that this "new normal" of not returning to the previous trend path of GDP is also evident in the actual and SPF forecast data in the aftermath of the 1991 and 2001 recessions. The "old normal" of a rapid return to the previous trend path is only evident after the 1981 recession.

It is interesting to note that when we compare the recent U.S. recovery to recoveries from the four previous post–WWII recessions, trend GDP growth across all five recoveries looks fairly similar in the first few quarters, but then we see evidence of a negative shock about a year into the recovery after the 1973, 1981, and 2008 downturns. However, instead of the quick reversal to stronger growth that we saw in the 1970s

Figure 6.7 U.S. Real GDP Forecast: Actual and Survey of Professional Forecasters, 1981–2011

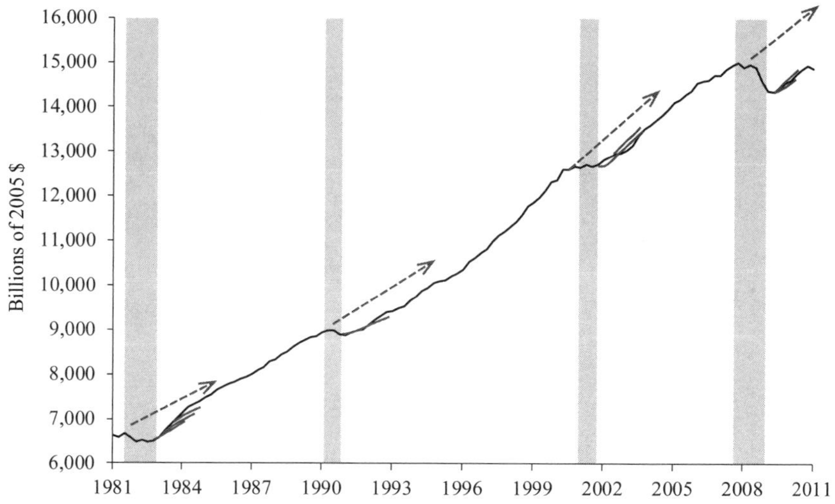

NOTE: Real GDP, billions of chained 2005 dollars, quarterly, seasonally adjusted (solid line), real-time Survey of Professional Forecasterss (dashed lines), trend growth (arrows). The SPF forecasts are made shortly after the preliminary release of data for the previous quarter.
SOURCE: Federal Reserve Bank of St. Louis.

and 1980s, Figure 6.8 shows that the recovery in the recent period never experiences a growth uptick. Table 6.1 provides a comparison of historical recoveries across the past 11 NBER-dated recessions. The Great Recession stands out for sustaining the largest 4-quarter GDP decline at the start of the recession, and the smallest GDP rise over the subsequent 10 quarters.

What might account for the unusually slow pace of the recovery after the Great Recession? One factor that the Congressional Budget Office (CBO) has emphasized is the concomitant reduction in potential GDP. "CBO estimates that about two-thirds of the difference between growth in real GDP in the current recovery and the average for other recoveries can be attributed to sluggish growth in potential GDP" (CBO 2012, pp. 2–3). Figure 6.9 shows actual real GDP starting in 2003 to the present, along with the precrisis trend, and CBO's estimate of potential GDP. The slower growth in potential GDP is, in turn, largely attributed to "long-term trends unrelated to the cycle, including the nation's chang-

Figure 6.8 U.S. Real GDP Recovery Comparisons

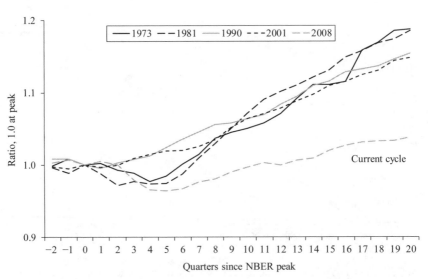

NOTE: Real GDP, billions of chained 2009 dollars, quarterly, seasonally adjusted annual rate. NBER business cycle dates: http://www.nber.org/cycles.html (accessed June 1, 2017).
SOURCE: Federal Reserve Bank of St. Louis.

Table 6.1 GDP Growth: Historical Recovery Comparisons

Recession		% change from peak at start of recession			
Start	End	4 quarters	8 quarters	12 quarters	14 quarters
Nov. 1948	Oct. 1949	−1.6	11.6	17.3	18.7
July 1953	May 1954	−2.2	5.2	7.5	9.1
Aug. 1957	April 1958	−0.9	6.0	8.4	7.7
April 1960	Feb. 1961	−1.0	6.4	10.3	13.8
Dec. 1969	Nov. 1970	0.4	9.2	14.5	14.6
Nov. 1973	March 1975	−2.0	0.5	4.8	8.1
Jan. 1980	July 1980	1.6	−0.9	0.6	4.9
July 1981	Nov. 1982	−2.7	2.8	9.8	11.8
July 1990	March 1991	−0.7	2.3	5.3	7.2
March 2001	Nov. 2001	1.5	3.3	7.3	9.0
Dec. 2007	June 2009	−3.3	−3.8	−0.8	−0.4
Average without recession of 2007–2009		−0.7	4.6	8.6	10.5

SOURCE: U.S. Bureau of Economic Analysis, National Bureau of Economic Research.

ing demographics" (CBO 2012, pp. 3). Past recoveries were helped by favorable demographic trends coming from increases in labor force participation of women and the strength of the baby boom, while the most recent recovery coincided with the retirement of baby boomers.

BUSINESS CYCLE COMOVEMENT

When America sneezes, the world catches cold—meaning, business cycles across the globe are increasingly synchronous with the U.S. cycle.[2] Ng and Wright (2013) provide an excellent survey of business cycle facts, updated to include the data from the Great Recession, and find strong evidence that recessions with financial market origins are different from those driven by supply or monetary policy shocks, and that when countries are more financially integrated, business cycles are more synchronous. In real business cycle models with complete markets, financially integrated economies will correlate negatively, leading to low synchronicity. However, if we (realistically) allow for the exis-

Figure 6.9 Great Recession GDP, Precrisis Trend, and CBO Potential GDP Estimate

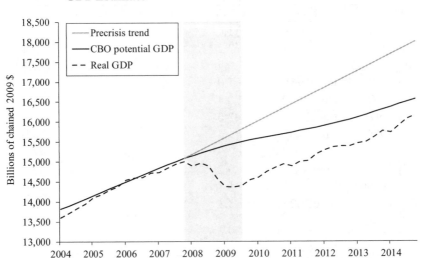

SOURCE: Federal Reserve Bank of St. Louis: Real GDP, billions of chained 2009 dollars, quarterly, seasonally adjusted annual rate; real potential GDP is the CBO's estimate of the output the economy would produce with a high rate of use of its capital and labor resources. The data are adjusted to remove the effects of inflation; trend line based on prerecession GDP growth.

tence of financial frictions that impede perfect risk sharing, business cycle models generally predict higher synchronicity when countries are more financially open and connected (Baxter and Crucini 1995).

Business cycle comovement is likely to increase when trade and financial linkages are stronger and policy responses are more similar. Figure 6.10 shows how U.S. trade volume (measured as imports plus exports as a share of GDP) has evolved over time; trade fell precipitously during the Great Recession, providing an important channel through which the downturn in the United States spread to the rest of the globe. However, the fact that trade volume bounced back to prerecession levels by early 2010 suggests that the trade channel is unlikely to be an important contributor to the slow global recovery. Cross-country holdings of assets grew dramatically in the early 2000s, and interestingly, while the rapid growth in foreign ownership of U.S. assets has largely returned to its prerecession trend line, the growth in U.S. hold-

Figure 6.10 U.S. Trade Linkages (share of trade in U.S. GDP)

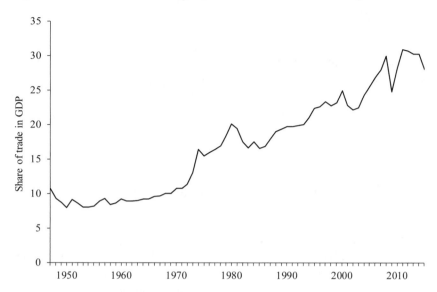

SOURCE: U.S. Bureau of Economic Analysis: Imports of Goods and Services plus Exports of Goods and Services over GDP.

ings of foreign assets has leveled off. This pattern tracks the recovery of global financial markets and returns; the U.S. recovery has been unusually slow, but the recovery in the rest of the globe has been even slower.

The timing of policy responses to the global downturn have also contributed to business cycle synchronicity. The European Central Bank held its target interest rate constant for a full year after the Fed started on its expansionary path, and initially it looked as if most developing countries would not be dragged down by the unfolding financial crisis in the advanced countries. By mid-2009, however, the Great Recession had become a global recession, and most countries followed the U.S. policy lead by implementing expansionary fiscal and monetary policy programs (Almunia et al. 2010). Toward the end of 2009 the U.S. economy looked as if it were on the brink of a robust rebound, and although the rest of the world was playing catch-up, economic forecasts were relatively optimistic for the global economy.[3] This upbeat forecast was fairly quickly reversed when the financial/fiscal problems in Europe began to be better understood. In 2011 global forecasts were substantially revised downward as a result of the combination of negative news from Japan due to the earthquake and tsunami, the euro-wide consequences of the ongoing debt crisis in Southern Europe, and the U.S. fiscal impasse, which led Standard and Poor's to downgrade U.S. government debt. Additional negative news continued in 2012, when the eurozone, the U.K., and Japan returned to recession; in 2013, when Cyprus and Portugal required bank bailouts and the U.S. government shut-down briefly; and in 2014, with Japan again returning to recession and the Russian Ruble crisis.

COMBINING NARRATIVE EVIDENCE WITH FORECASTS

Real-time economic forecasts provide high-frequency information about the perceived state of the economy based on available data. Likewise, narrative information from contemporaneous news reports and government announcements help to identify the policy and financial market shocks to the global economy that potentially influenced the forecasts. Dominguez and Shapiro (2013) follow in the tradition of Ramey and Shapiro (1998) and Romer and Romer (2010) to combine forecast revisions with narrative information in the years immediately following the Great Recession to better understand the reasons for the slow U.S. recovery. They argue that the U.S. recovery from the Great Recession was stalled in 2010, 2011, and 2012 by negative shocks mainly emanating from Europe. Table 6.2 updates the narrative evidence through 2014 and includes a broader group of countries in the analysis. Whereas most news concerning the Great Recession is centered on the United States in 2008–2009, the focus shifts to the eurozone starting in 2010, to Asia in 2011, and to Russia in 2014.

Table 6.3 documents the revisions in the two-year cumulative economic outlook for 14 countries over the period 2009–2014 using the IMF's World Economic Outlook forecasts. These forecast revisions in the IMF's outlook for the United States align well with the narrative evidence summarized in Table 6.2. Negative shocks from Europe, Asia, and Russia led to substantial downward revisions in growth prospects for countries in these regions, and these shocks also seem to have adversely impacted the outlook for the United States.

Table 6.2 Percent of Occurrences of Recession-Related Policy and Financial Market News Events

Year	U.S. news	Asia news	U.K. & Russia news	Eurozone news
2008	55	10	11	24
2009	52	15	10	23
2010	33	2	3	62
2011	13	20	2	65
2012	8	21	6	65
2013	20	11	7	62
2014	9	18	27	45

SOURCE: *Financial Times*, *Wall Street Journal*, BBC News, Federal Reserve websites, U.S. Treasury, European Central Bank, European Commission.

CONCLUSIONS

The slow recovery from the Great Recession has lowered prospective standards of living for people in the United States and around the world. The consequences of the high levels of unemployment, especially for those who were just starting their working careers when the recession hit, are likely to be felt for many decades to come. Older workers whose savings and pension plans were devastated by the financial crisis are unlikely to ever recuperate those losses. Moreover, the slow pace of recovery in business investment, worker productivity, and consumer confidence suggests that even those not directly hit by the recession will be affected. It is difficult to fully explain these outcomes based only on U.S. economic conditions, even if we consider the precipitating financial crisis and CBO's estimates of the reduction in potential GDP. The international dimension of the weak recovery is unsurprising given the complex interdependencies of the global economy. The 2008 financial crisis started in the United States but soon spread around the globe. The aftershocks from this crisis and the subsequent Great Recession continue to reverberate in Europe, Asia, and Russia, along with their own homegrown economic crises. These combined shocks in turn have prolonged and weakened the global recovery.

Table 6.3 Revision in Two-Year Cumulative GDP Growth Outlook

	U.S.	Cyprus	France	Germany	Greece	Nether-lands	Portugal	Spain	Korea	Japan	Iceland	U.K.	Russia	China
2009	3.2	-2.6	1.0	2.7	1.1	2.7	1.8	-0.1	4.1	2.3	-3.6	2.6	2.1	3.1
2010	-0.5	-0.2	-0.2	0.5	-3.1	0.7	-1.4	-0.3	-1.1	-0.9	1.4	-1.0	2.1	-0.6
2011	-2.2	-2.4	-0.8	-1.6	-6.1	-0.3	-2.7	-1.0	0.3	0.5	-0.7	-1.5	-0.9	-1.0
2012	-0.5	-3.5	-1.8	-1.2	-7.9	-0.9	-2.7	-2.9	-0.7	-0.9	0	-1.8	-0.2	-1.1
2013	-0.7	n/a	0.2	-0.1	0.1	-1.5	0.3	-1.1	-0.4	-0.3	0	0.7	-1.6	-2.0

NOTE: Revisions from the second to fourth quarter of the forecast for the cumulative percent change real GDP two years ahead.
SOURCE: IMF World Economic Outlook reports, April 2009–October 2014.

Notes

1. See also Romer and Romer (2015), who argue that output declines following financial crises are highly variable and depend importantly on the severity and persistence of the financial distress itself.
2. This is thought to be a modern adaptation of a nineteenth century saying attributed to Austria's Prince Clemens von Metternich, originally: "When France sneezes all Europe catches a cold."
3. See the IMF's World Economic Outlook forecasts for 2009 in Table 6.3.

References

Almunia, Miguel, Agustín Bénétrix, Barry Eichengreen, Kevin H. O'Rourke, and Gisela Rua. 2010. "From Great Depression to Great Credit Crisis: Similarities, Differences and Lessons." *Economic Policy* 25(62): 219–265.

Baxter, Marianne, and Mario J. Crucini. 1995. "Business Cycles and the Asset Structure of Foreign Trade." *International Economic Review* 36(4): 821–854.

Brown, E. Cay. 1956. "Fiscal Policy in the 'Thirties: A Reappraisal." *American Economic Review* 46(5): 857–879.

Congressional Budget Office (CBO). 2012. What Accounts for the Slow Growth of the Economy after the Recession? Washington, DC: CBO. https://www.cbo.gov/publication/43707 (accessed April 27, 2017).

DeLong, J. Bradford. 1998. "Fiscal Policy in the Shadow of the Great Depression." In *The Defining Moment: The Great Depression and the American Economy in the Twentieth Century*, Michael D. Bordo, Claudia Goldin, and Eugene N. White, eds. Chicago: University of Chicago Press, pp. 67–86. http://www.nber.org/chapters/c6888.pdf (accessed April 27, 2017).

Dominguez, Kathryn M. E., Ray Fair, and Matthew Shapiro. 1998. "Forecasting the Depression: Harvard versus Yale." *American Economic Review* 78(4): 595–612.

Dominguez, Kathryn M. E., and Matthew Shapiro. 2013. "Forecasting the Recovery from the Great Recession: Is This Time Different?" *American Economic Review: Papers and Proceedings* 103(3): 147–152.

Friedman, Milton, and Anna Jacobson Schwartz. 1963. *A Monetary History of the United States, 1867–1960*. Princeton, NJ: Princeton University Press.

Hausman, Joshua. 2016. "Fiscal Policy and Economic Recovery: The Case of the 1936 Veterans' Bonus." *American Economic Review* 106(4): 1100–1143.

Ho, Giang, and Paolo Mauro. 2014. "Growth: Now and Forever?" IMF Working Paper No. 14/117. Washington, DC: International Monetary Fund.

International Monetary Fund (IMF). 2008–2014. *World Economic Outlook Database*. Washington, DC: IMF.

Keynes, John Maynard. 1936. *The General Theory of Employment, Interest, and Money*. London: Macmillan.

Ng, Serena, and Jonathan H. Wright. 2013. "Facts and Challenges from the Great Recession for Forecasting and Macroeconomic Modeling." *Journal of Economic Literature* 51(4): 1120–1154.

Potter, Simon. 2011. "The Failure to Forecast the Great Recession." *Liberty Street Economics* (blog), Federal Reserve Bank of New York, November 25. http://libertystreeteconomics.newyorkfed.org/2011/11/the-failure-to-forecast-the-great-recession.html#.V4P4t_krJaQ (accessed June 1, 2017).

Ramey, Valerie A., and Matthew D. Shapiro. 1998. "Costly Capital Reallocation and the Effects of Government Spending." *Carnegie Rochester Conference on Public Policy* 48: 145–194.

Reinhart, Carmen M., and Kenneth S. Rogoff. 2011. *This Time Is Different: Eight Centuries of Financial Folly*. Princeton, NJ: Princeton University Press.

———. 2014. "Recovery from Financial Crises: Evidence from 100 Episodes." *American Economic Review: Papers and Proceedings* 104(5): 50–55.

Romer, Christina D. 1992. "What Ended the Great Depression?" *Journal of Economic History* 52(4): 757–784.

Romer, Christina, and David Romer. 2010. "The Macroeconomic Effects of Tax Changes: Estimates Bases on a New Measure of Fiscal Shocks." *American Economic Review* 100(3): 763–801.

———. 2015. "New Evidence on the Impact of Financial Crises in Advanced Countries." NBER Working Paper No. 21021. Cambridge, MA: National Bureau of Economic Research.

Temin, Peter. 1989. *Lessons from the Great Depression*. Cambridge, MA: MIT Press.

Authors

Eskander Alvi is a professor of economics at Western Michigan University.

Laurence Ball is department chair and a professor of economics at Johns Hopkins University.

Gary Burtless is a senior fellow and holds the John C. and Nancy D. Whitehead Chair in Economic Studies at the Brookings Institution.

J. Bradford DeLong is a professor of economics at the University of California–Berkeley.

Kathryn M.E. Dominguez is a professor of public policy and economics at the University of Michigan and research associate at the National Bureau of Economic Research.

Barry Eichengreen is the George C. Pardee and Helen N. Pardee Professor of Economics and Political Science at the University of California–Berkeley.

Donald Kohn holds the Robert V. Roosa Chair in International Economics and is a senior fellow in the Economic Studies program at the Brookings Institution.

Lawrence H. Summers is the Charles W. Eliot University Professor and president emeritus of Harvard University.

Index

Note: The italic letters *f, n,* or *t* following a page number indicate a figure, note, or table, respectively, on that page. Double letters mean more than one such consecutive item on a single page.

About the Institute

The W.E. Upjohn Institute for Employment Research is a nonprofit research organization devoted to finding and promoting solutions to employment-related problems at the national, state, and local levels. It is an activity of the W.E. Upjohn Unemployment Trustee Corporation, which was established in 1932 to administer a fund set aside by Dr. W.E. Upjohn, founder of The Upjohn Company, to seek ways to counteract the loss of employment income during economic downturns.

The Institute is funded largely by income from the W.E. Upjohn Unemployment Trust, supplemented by outside grants, contracts, and sales of publications. Activities of the Institute comprise the following elements: 1) a research program conducted by a resident staff of professional social scientists; 2) a competitive grant program, which expands and complements the internal research program by providing financial support to researchers outside the Institute; 3) a publications program, which provides the major vehicle for disseminating the research of staff and grantees, as well as other selected works in the field; and 4) an Employment Management Services division, which manages most of the publicly funded employment and training programs in the local area.

The broad objectives of the Institute's research, grant, and publication programs are to 1) promote scholarship and experimentation on issues of public and private employment and unemployment policy, and 2) make knowledge and scholarship relevant and useful to policymakers in their pursuit of solutions to employment and unemployment problems.

Current areas of concentration for these programs include causes, consequences, and measures to alleviate unemployment; social insurance and income maintenance programs; compensation; workforce quality; work arrangements; family labor issues; labor-management relations; and regional economic development and local labor markets.